Collective Bargaining:
New Dimensions in Labor Relations

Other Titles of Interest

Know-How on the Job: The Important Knowledge of "Unskilled Workers," Ken C. Kusterer

Working Women: A Study of Women in Paid Jobs, edited by Ann Seidman

A Westview Special Study

Collective Bargaining:
New Dimensions in Labor Relations
edited by Franklin J. Havelick

This analysis of the changing process of union-employer collective bargaining represents the first-person views of some of the most prominent figures in U.S. labor relations. Based on a series of addresses and discussions at the Institute of Collective Bargaining, each part of the book contains two chapters that sharply contrast the views of representatives of labor, business, government, and other "third parties." The contributors discuss fundamental domestic and international economic and political trends, as well as the most salient contemporary issues, including inflation, unemployment, automation, productivity, foreign trade, multinational corporations, government intervention, and worker alienation.

Franklin J. Havelick is deputy counsel to New York City's Mayor Edward I. Koch and assistant professor of public affairs at Columbia University. Previously he was an attorney with the firm of Battle, Fowler, Jaffin, Pierce & Kheel, specializing in litigation and labor law.

Collective Bargaining:
New Dimensions in Labor Relations

edited by Franklin J. Havelick
Foreword by Theodore W. Kheel

A Giniger Project Published by
Westview Press, Boulder, Colorado

A Westview Special Study

Copyright © 1979 by the Institute of Collective Bargaining and Group Relations, Inc.

Published in association with The K. S. Giniger Company in 1979 in the United States of America by
  Westview Press, Inc.
  5500 Central Avenue
  Boulder, Colorado 80301
  Frederick A. Praeger, Publisher

Library of Congress Cataloging in Publication Data
Main entry under title:
Collective Bargaining.
  (A Westview special study)
  Includes index.
  1. Collective bargaining—United States—Addresses, essays, lectures. 2. Collective bargaining—Addresses, essays, lectures. I. Havelick, Franklin J.
HD6508.C657   331.89'0973   79-4234
ISBN 0-89158-386-6

Printed and bound in the United States of America

Contents

Foreword

It is a pleasure to write an opening to this remarkable volume on collective bargaining, which contains chapters by some of the art's most prominent practitioners. Their first-person analyses of the collective bargaining system comprise a unique work: no such book now exists or is likely to be published soon.

Collective Bargaining: New Dimensions in Labor Relations is the product of several years of interesting activity at the Institute of Collective Bargaining and Group Relations located at Automation House in New York City. It is the Institute's purpose to foster understanding of collective bargaining as the only viable means of resolving the dynamics of labor-management relations in a democratic society. Toward this end it has offered a program of addresses and seminars for unionists, managers, lawyers, academics, the press, and government officials. The program, supported by a grant from the Ford Foundation and by many contributions, was presented in cooperation with the New York State School of Industrial and Labor Relations at Cornell University.

Each of the ten chapters of this book was drawn from remarks delivered at the Institute over a period of two years (1976-77). The authors originally argued their theses before an audience of peers prone to examine all premises and to challenge conclusions when they seemed vulnerable. The proceedings were recorded, transcribed, edited, and rewritten for the present collection. As a result, I believe they have in common a pointed quality—a clarity of interest and argument—unusual in published writing by public figures.

Collective bargaining is so much a personal process that the views and attitudes of the participants may well determine the effectiveness of the process. The characters of the negotiators will unavoidably affect the outcome of the bargaining. The primary source materials that make up the book, together with the contributors' biographies, provide many insights into the personal dimension of collective bargaining.

However, no print portrait of the authors can adequately describe their vivid individual personalities. In writing this preface, I recall the wonderful variety of their appearances at the Institute: Bill Winpisinger's roaring defense of labor's productivity; Malcolm Denise's cool, analytical interpretation of international labor economics; and Jerry Rosow's inspired vision of a more participatory, fulfilling work life.

The general style of these essays is in good measure attributable to their editor, Franklin Havelick, who conceived the book, then prepared, researched, and revised its contents. In 1976 Frank, at that time my associate in law practice, received a Ford Foundation Fellowship in collective bargaining. He undertook a wide variety of efforts to study as well as teach collective bargaining. He completed a master's thesis in labor policy at Columbia University, and he has commenced a doctoral dissertation on public sector labor relations. He is now deputy counsel to New York City's Mayor Edward I. Koch and assistant professor of public affairs at Columbia University.

As a former labor lawyer and a political scientist, and more recently as a government official, Frank Havelick is well qualified to have created this book. *Collective Bargaining* describes a system for resolving economic and political conflict that is itself subject to external pressures that cause manifold changes in the bargaining system. The book is broad enough to encompass some of the more fundamental questions—productivity, inflation, and unemployment, for example—while examining specific issues such as the cost-of-living adjustment and the multinational corporation. By pairing chapters by authors from labor and management, or from other divergent backgrounds, Frank provides us with sharp contrasts, like the discussions of political activities of public employee unions. Thus, the content of the book, which has been admirably edited and indexed, is enhanced by its structure.

Collective Bargaining is an essential book for those interested in the current theory and practice of labor relations. It is, moreover, a book that will help both employees and employers, as well as students, the press, and public officials, to understand collective bargaining in terms of the future of industrial peace and democracy.

Theodore W. Kheel

Acknowledgments

During the three years (1976 to 1978) I spent editing this book, I received support in different ways from a great number of people. Their interest and generosity sustained my efforts and gave them purpose. I am glad to have this chance to thank them.

Ted Kheel was the sponsor of my work on this book and my mentor as a labor lawyer. I had no intention of practicing labor law when I joined his firm in 1973. The force of his personality and intellect directed my interests in law, politics, and social problems toward labor litigation and collective bargaining. He and his partner, Dick Adelman, taught me to write a brief, to make an oral argument, to represent the interests of both labor and management, and to act as a neutral third party. Few lawyers have been as fortunate in their early training.

Penny Panoulias, administrative director of the book project, handled preliminary research, transcription of tape recordings, supervision of secretarial work, and preparation of the manuscript. She worked long hours after her own day's work to see the project to completion, and throughout remained the most capable and whimsical of colleagues.

Mike Sviridoff and Stan Brezenoff of the Ford Foundation granted a fellowship that permitted this long-term research and writing project, which included a speakers program and graduate study. Charles Hamilton, Alan Westin, Richard Rubin, and Bruce Vladeck of the Columbia University political science department have been my professors in the fields of public policy and political economy, as well as my advisors on matters academic and otherwise.

Herbert Bienstock and Martin Karlin of the United States Bureau of Labor Statistics provided a wealth of empirical data for the statistical appendix. The charts and tables were prepared by artist and designer John Yue, with typography by Dunung Tjokronolo. Patricia Ruggieri, Grace Araujo, and Joseph Osenni, administrative assistants for the project, as well as the staff and typists of the Institute of Collective Bargaining, and Ken Giniger, the book agent, all helped the project to bear fruit.

I would like to take this opportunity to express my thanks to Mayor Edward I. Koch, in whose administration I am honored to serve, and to my colleagues in New York City government. My work on the book was completed at City Hall at the same time, ironically, as I began an apprenticeship in public sector labor relations.

Finally, I am grateful for the profound contribution to this book made by my parents, Raymond and Rosalia, to whom it is dedicated.

Franklin J. Havelick

Collective Bargaining:
New Dimensions in Labor Relations

Introduction

Franklin J. Havelick

"We've got to have a whole lot of changes in this contract or our men will shut the damn mill down until we get them. We're looking for a sizable increase in wages and premium pay, an end to this business of contracting out when our members are getting laid off, and the alcoholism rehabilitation program we talked about last time." Having made his points, the sixty-year-old representative from the Steelworkers International pushed the union's list of demands a few inches forward. Then he laid both of his large, reddish arms on the table and leveled a resolute look at the independent steel company's chief negotiator across from him. The young, newly elected president of the local union sat back in his chair, slowly chewing tobacco. The other members of the union's negotiating committee casually scanned the faces of the management team for reactions.

"Well, Jim, that's what I came down here to Kentucky to talk to you about," replied the labor relations manager of the parent company that owns the steel mill. "You know we've got our own problems keeping up with the Japanese and one of those problems is the way we've got the melt shop set up. If we can't get some cooperation from you on reducing the furnace crew from three men a shift to two, we'll have to start looking for places to cut back. I think we can work something out on premium pay and some of these other items, but we're not going to make work for your guys when we can contract it out for a fraction of the cost."

The local president held a cup to his mouth and let go of some tobacco juice. The company's spokesman, an intense, athletic man in his late forties, passed a note to the older man on his right, the plant manager, who read it, looked at his watch, then spoke in a low chuckle. "Before we take a little break here, I wonder if I ever told you boys about old Calvin Headrick. Didn't give a tinker's damn for the new gauges and tests when they first came in. Said they only confused the issue. Calvin would stand in front of the furnace with his hands in his pockets, staring down into the ladle, clicking his teeth. He always knew when it was time to pour just by watching. I swear he did it by counting the clicks."

*　　*　　*

I was privileged to have played a supporting role in this scene as the company's counsel. After some four months of bargaining, the parties reached agreement on a new contract. Perhaps never again will collective bargaining seem so clearly to me a noble and necessary process of tactical cooperation. The period 1968-77 was affected by strongly conflicting social and political pressures, as well as adverse economic forces. The collective bargaining system was reshaped by those forces in a fashion not yet clear. This book seeks to describe the new system in terms of its major dimensions in the words of those who see it from within.

In addition to storytelling and "chewing," I learned from those steel negotiations just how complex collective bargaining has become in the last ten years (1968-77). The steel industry, like much of the economy, has been troubled in recent times by foreign competition and weak demand. Layoffs and plant closings have brought management and union counter-charges of featherbedding and mismanagement. The response to these conditions by the "Big Steel" companies and the

Steelworkers Union has been industry bargaining on a new labor relations framework, including cost-of-living adjustments, an expedited arbitration procedure, and an Experimental Negotiating Agreement for the elimination of strikes.

Steel is a concentrated industry dominated by a few large producers and organized principally by a single union. Local bargaining, particularly in smaller steel companies, is still very important. It includes a broadening range of new subjects, such as employee alcoholism, and the particular solutions to problems created by changing patterns of investment and competition, training and technology.

The traditional bargaining subjects have been wages, hours, and basic working conditions. However, wage bargaining has been greatly complicated by economic and other forces during the last decade, most importantly simultaneous inflation and recession. These conditions have resulted in strong wage demands, despite high unemployment and employer resistance based on depressed economic growth.

During the 1968-77 period, average weekly earnings of production workers and the consumer price index both rose at an average rate of about 6.5 percent a year, so that little or no real wage gains were realized. Hourly output for the same period was nearly constant, increasing at an average annual rate of about only 2 percent, while unemployment averaged 6 percent.

Horvitz and Winpisinger

It is little wonder then that Wayne Horvitz begins his essay on the state of the collective bargaining system by quoting "the Ol' Perfesser," Casey Stengel: "Can't anybody here play this game?" The players may very well not know the rules, since they have been changing quickly and inconsistently. From the historical perspective of the chief federal mediator, Horvitz sees collective bargaining as a social system that has not yet adapted to the changing conditions of the last decade, but which is inherently viable because it is essentially voluntary and improvisational.

Although there are about 172 major unions and nearly 200,000 collective bargaining agreements, Horvitz discerns a decline in collective bargaining and a coincidental rise in government regulatory agencies with jurisdiction over labor relations. He believes this trend is the result of failing confidence in union leaders and corporate managers and concludes that there is a need for continuing reliance on adversarial collective bargaining and the development of new cooperative labor-management procedures with the assistance of third party neutrals. Horvitz cites two experimental arrangements concerning automation and wage-price controls in which he has participated as examples of such cooperative procedures. Many of Horvitz's points recur throughout the book, although with different inferences drawn by different authors.

William Winpisinger's companion chapter on the state of the system is primarily concerned with productivity as an objective measure of the social utility of collective bargaining. Winpisinger, an iconoclastic union president, argues that there is no need to supplant or to supplement the collective bargaining system with such cooperative schemes as the Kelso Plan or codetermination to improve worker satisfaction. He also rejects the use of third parties as largely unnecessary to productive labor relations.

Winpisinger maintains that increasing labor costs have stimulated the use of labor-saving devices and, therefore, improved productivity. Since technology is necessary to higher living standards, organized labor does not oppose automation or computerization. He argues that higher wages, shorter work weeks, and improved conditions all contribute to productivity, as do apprenticeship programs and arbitration procedures. Winpisinger's ultimate conclusion is that collective bargaining is necessary to assure increased productivity and must be expanded.

Kheel and Watts

Two major aspects of the economic dimension of the collective bargaining system, automation and inflation, are discussed by Theodore Kheel and Glenn Watts in microeconomic and macroeconomic analyses, respectively. Kheel's description of the technological revolution in the newspaper industry spans the last fifteen years, beginning with the 1963 New York newspaper strike and ending with a foreshadowing of the 1978 strike.

In opposition to Winpisinger's view, Kheel asserts that automation presents a fundamental conflict between the most crucial of labor and management interests. To the employer, automation represents "the promise of competitive advantages"—higher output, economies of scale, and lower labor costs per unit. To the employee, it represents "a threat to job security" and, in some instances, to an entire craft or profession. However, Kheel believes that to the extent that labor and management have a common interest in the employer's competitiveness, collective bargaining offers a framework for the orderly introduction of labor-saving technology, an analysis shared by Sol Chaikin in a later chapter.

Kheel demonstrates his point by recounting the introduction of "cold type" in newspapers, where the Typographers Union was faced with a choice "between zero union members doing composing work or 50, . . . (as against 500 that might have been [formerly] required). Not being a silly man, [the union president] agreed" to 50. Where automated competition threatens an entire industry, the union cannot resist the introduction of new technology.

The revolutionary 1974 newspaper agreement on automation required eleven years of mediated bargaining. The process resulted in a contract that, according to Kheel, fully satisfied both the union's goal of preserving jobs permanently and management's goal of introducing new equipment freely.

While collective bargaining may have thereby resolved an
intractable issue for some papers, Kheel acknowledges that
others have claimed collective bargaining prevented publishers
from reducing labor inefficiency at the majority of the New
York City papers that eventually failed.

However, Kheel, a labor lawyer and mediator, says that such
dislocations are basically attributable to external forces that
labor and management have only limited ability to control.
Perhaps a clearer example of an externality that shapes
collective bargaining, but is beyond the control of bargainers at
the company or industry level, is inflation.

For just that reason, Glenn Watts's analysis of inflation is
framed generally in the contemporary political rhetoric of the
union movement, instead of adhering to the technical and
historical details of Kheel's essay. As a union president, Watts
sees inflation as an enormous external force, overwhelming the
negotiator's agreement and the workers' wage gains. Indeed, in
the last ten years there has been no significant increase in real
wages. Watts points out that "a dollar in pension benefits
negotiated in 1970 may literally not be worth a nickel by 1985."

Watts describes federal fiscal and monetary policies, as well
as trade deficits and other international events, as setting in
motion inflationary reactions that are impossible to anticipate
or take into account. The problem, Watts declares, has been
compounded by coincidental periods of recession and inflation, or "stagflation." Among the devices unions have proposed under these circumstances are the shorter work week and
the guaranteed annual wage to offset both declining real income and decreasing job security.

In the face of workers' concerns that collective bargaining
may not be able to protect them from inflation and often bitter
dissatisfaction with their work, Watts says "the labor
movement must look to the political system for relief." Since a
legislated tax cut is the equivalent of a negotiated wage
increase, Watts views the political context of collective
bargaining in broad terms that include employment programs and national health insurance, both of which may

have anti-inflationary effects.

Bailar and Shanker

The interrelationship of the political process and the collective bargaining system is analyzed in narrower terms by Benjamin Bailar and Albert Shanker, both parties to public employee bargaining. As Watts implies, Shanker declares that lobbying and elective campaigns have become necessary to reach goals no longer achievable within the bargaining system.

Shanker has had long experience with the political system as a precursor of, and then as an alternative to, the bargaining system. His current views directly conflict with his own position a decade ago: when teachers were seeking bargaining rights and wage increases, Shanker and the other "Young Turks" of the United Federation of Teachers believed that the two systems were mutually exclusive.

Former Postmaster General Ben Bailar sees the political system as disruptive of orderly labor relations, which require that the roles of manager and union leader be clearly defined and played with equal vigor. Where labor, or presumably management, has disproportionate power in the political determination of wages or working conditions, the advantaged party, according to Bailar, has inevitably used force to achieve its sometimes irrational ends.

Bailar and Shanker separately relate the evolution of postal and teacher labor relations in three historical phases, which may be characterized as political, nonpolitical, and mixed. Both perceive a trend toward repoliticization, which they suggest will strengthen the bargaining position of public unions, but which they view with the opposing interests of labor and management.

Bailar recalls the 1970 postal strike as the catalyst for reorganizing the post office as a public cooperation with the right to collective bargaining, but not with the right to strike. Shanker recalls the illegal 1968 New York City teachers' strike against decentralization of the school system as the stimulus for renewing the union's political activism.

The varying interpretations of similar or identical facts apparent in the Watts, Shanker, and Bailar essays are not only the result of labor-management antagonism; they also reflect a multiplicity of subtler interests and values that color perceptions differently depending on the individual's background and vantage point. Labor leaders Watts and Winpisinger have opposing views on the satisfaction of union members with the quality of their working life. Shanker, who once opposed political participation by his union, now favors it. Many employers oppose no-layoff agreements like the ones favored by Watts, but Bailar approved such a provision in return for a no-strike clause; and, in the summer of 1978, postal management unsuccessfully sought to eliminate that clause. There are many shadings of opinion, and very little of it in black and white, regarding the major collective bargaining issues discussed throughout this book.

Chaikin and Denise

Sol Chaikin is the president of the Ladies Garment Workers Union, which represents employees located mainly in the New York metropolitan area, but which is actively organizing throughout the United States in response to domestic and international economic conditions. This triple perspective is increasingly common and is shared by Malcolm Denise, the former vice-president for labor relations of Ford Motor Company.

Chaikin's principal argument is that international economic forces destabilize collective bargaining. Denise's diametrically opposed conclusion is that they tend to rationalize the allocation of labor and capital and, therefore, to stabilize the larger collective bargaining system. Chaikin describes the geographic dispersion of his industry and the expansion of foreign competition as independent developments motivated by a common interest in obtaining cheap labor with the common result of disorganizing the labor market. In certain respects, Chaikin's analysis of national and international economics parallels Shanker's analysis of local and national political forces.

In response to the prevailing adverse economic conditions in the garment industry, Chaikin determined that his union would "do everything possible to maintain the market position of the employers in the metropolitan area" who operate "older, less efficient plants." To maintain its organization, the union took the lead in creating mechanisms for improving employer productivity through collective bargaining. The union developed sliding pay scales and productivity bonuses, training and mechanization programs—actions comparable to those taken by the newspaper publishers.

Because garment manufacturing is labor-intensive, the Garment Workers Union has strongly supported protectionist trade legislation. Automobile manufacturing is technology-intensive, but nevertheless sensitive to rising foreign competition. Since Ford has affiliates operating in thirty countries, it views supranational economies of scale and the organization of national labor markets in terms of finding "the best ways to sell Ford products in the world's markets." For this purpose Ford has adopted differing bargaining positions throughout the world as required by each domestic bargaining system encountered. In some countries, Ford has bargained individually, while in others it has participated in group or industry-wide bargaining, but it has never bargained on a multinational basis with a federation of trade unions. In this manner Ford seeks to optimize its labor costs and output.

Green and Rosow

Denise foresees the future development of macrobargaining units as a result of the progressive internationalization of industry, although he does not believe such a bargaining system has yet been demonstrated to be useful to American management. Chaikin believes management in his industry will continue to bargain in small units. How the structure of collective bargaining is evolving at this time is more difficult to determine than the issues that will shape the system. In this respect the last two chapters by Ernest Green and Jerome Rosow, who have both served as assistant secretary of labor, represent contrasting but complementary interpretations of the social questions that will be discussed across the bargaining table.

Green argues that the scope of the bargaining system must be enlarged to permit labor and management to take part in the resolution of continuing unemployment, much of it structural in the sense that it is the result of the organization of the labor market. Without the cooperation of the labor and management institutions that dominate that market, it will be difficult, he asserts, to implement the two major employment programs: public service employment and job training. Affirmative action, minimum wage, and industry subsidy legislation also require support from both labor and management.

Rosow believes "the new issues on the bargaining table are remarkably qualitative, rather than the largely quantitative concern with higher wages which workers have expressed in the past." Instead of "more," the future goal of labor will be "better." Like Winpisinger, Rosow is convinced that the quality of working life and productivity are linked. Improving the quality of the employee's work life, like increasing the use of automation, may well result in greater output.

But while Rosow sees codetermination, productivity sharing, and other cooperative labor-management schemes as compatible with collective bargaining, Winpisinger does not. For Winpisinger, quantitative changes—increased wages and greater automation—lead to a higher standard of living and improve the quality of work.

The Art of Bargaining

As a member of the board of directors of Rosow's Work in

America Institute, Bill Winpisinger has had frequent opportunities to disagree with Jerry Rosow. They and the other contributors to this book also argued the points made in this book before audiences at the Institute of Collective Bargaining. Through respectful editing, I have tried to retain the lively colors in which those views were originally expressed. I have also provided biographical and statistical appendixes to shed further light on the participants and their arguments, with the statistical material organized in the same sequence as the chapters of the book.

At Automation House, the Institute has on display a George Segal sculpture, in the form of two men arm wrestling, portraying collective bargaining. As Ben Bailar notes in Chapter 5, the Postal Service has issued a stamp bearing a symbolic representation of the sculpture: two opposing arrows in a unified design. Both the sculpture and the stamp bear the legend "Out of Conflict—Accord."

This book is to me a further abstraction of the tumult of labor relations described by Wayne Horvitz. It is a series of responses to the great events of the last ten years of collective bargaining, arranged in different configurations. The patterns of the chapters, laid one over another like transparent planes, present a composite picture of the new dimensions of collective bargaining.

Part 1
The State of the System

jurisdiction over occupational safety and health (OSHA), pensions (ERISA), equal employment (EEOC), and through the courts. These governmental initiatives are a direct reflection and affirmation of the fact that people are discontented with pensions, health plans, the quality of working life, and the work place itself. Despite the counter-vailing political pressures to which the federal government is subject and the diffusion of power among Congress, the executive branch, and the courts, there has been concerted action to create and to enforce these laws during Republican and Democratic administrations.

The reaction of labor and management has been shock and occasionally intransigent opposition. Institutionalization is, I recognize, often desirable to those who have become comfor-table with prevailing arrangements, but those who would preserve the status quo in collective bargaining seek to attach permanency to something that was never meant to be permanent. When Walter Reuther and Charlie Wilson got their heads together and talked about the collective bargaining agreement as a living document, they were recognizing the need for flexibility and adaptation in a process in which they were partners. Institutional preservation not only occupies the time and energy of labor and management—resources that could be spent more creatively—it also tends to distort the essential nature of collective bargaining and to prevent its enrichment through the testing of new ideas. Management's great cry is "Don't interfere in our organization." The outcome of this stonewalling attitude is that the creative potential of the process, and particularly the effective use of third parties, is obstructed.

On the management side, it has long been my fear (and the conduct of the J. P. Stevens Company is just the tip of the iceberg) that most American managers have never really accepted the trade union movement as necessary to our kind of democratic industrial system. They reluctantly accept the unions as adversaries and they understand the responsibilities of unions and management under the law, but fundamentally they follow what I have come to call "Dover's Law." I learned Dover's Law from an associate who was a production supervisor in a plant where I worked many years ago. It was George Dover's belief that if he was good to his wife and children all week and went to church on Sunday, on Monday when he came to the plant the union would be gone. (Dover's Law had many corollaries.)

Such stubborn devotion to Dover's Law has led management to fruitless confrontations and an almost blindly legalist approach to labor relations. Unions have responded by hiring their own batteries of lawyers, in an effort to readjust the balance of power in collective bargaining. As the law proliferates, so does participation by and reliance upon lawyers. There is an endless series of amendments to the "Lawyers' Full Employment Act." If management finds the NLRB such a burden, it has mostly itself to blame. Thirty years after the passage of the Taft-Hartley Law, which was an attempt to redress the labor-management balance in management's favor, the tenacity of Dover's Law is demonstrated by the fact that the greatest number of cases coming before the board involve union recognition, and cases involving the duty to bargain are close behind.

Indeed it is tragic that there is still widespread unwillingness on the part of management to accept unions and to work within the collective bargaining framework in order to achieve greater communication and cooperation on matters of mutual interest. There is nothing wrong with the adversary relationship. On the contrary, it is necessary to shape the forces that make collective bargaining productive. But there are issues that, because of their nature and complexity, have to be attacked in other ways, and it is the responsibility of the labor-management community to sort out which procedures are appropriate to which problems.

I have been part of two experiments that I believe show what can be done when the collective bargaining system is opened up to new procedures. The first experiment produced the mechanization and modernization agreement on the West Coast docks; the second involved my more recent tenure as chairman of the joint labor-management committee for the retail food industry. The agreement that led to the formation of the food industry committee was not the product of a fit of altruism and concern for the public. It grew from the shattering experience of twenty-two months of government wage and price controls that neither side wanted to recur. With the help of third parties like John Dunlop and William Usery, labor and management reached an agreement to form the committee, which has not only survived but has actually helped ameliorate some of the food industry's difficulties.

It is often said that experiments like the food industry committee are examples of big management and big labor getting together to victimize the public and that in the end the public will pay for this kind of cooperation or partnership. Critics fear that the unions will continue to demand larger and larger shares of corporate earnings and that the companies will respond by passing costs on to the consumer. While the outcome of such arrangements may be uncertain, the pressures that led to the committee's formation do not lead me to this conclusion. Food industry management is necessarily concerned about consumer demands, and labor fears the encroachments of non-union competition, whose pressures they would be foolish to ignore.

The horrified cries over big labor and big business getting together to do in the public have a familiar ring from a totally different quarter. I remember when the organized Left of this country pilloried Harry Bridges, then president of the International Longshoremen and Warehousemen's Union, for having sold out the workers by making the union a partner in the creation of the mechanization fund on the West Coast waterfront in the early sixties. I do not know whether Bridges sold out his members, but I do know what happened in the ensuing years. The dialogue and cooperation that Bridges helped initiate made it possible for the parties to solve some seemingly intractable problems. The cooperative elements of this relationship are still in existence, the adversary elements of collective bargaining remain, and the process is thriving under a new and younger leadership. The interests of the longshore-men on the West Coast and in Hawaii will continue to be pressed by a vigorous union while the shipping industry benefits from containerization and other advances in produc-tivity.

I also believe that the federal government should participate with labor and management in cooperative dispute settlement procedures to extend the scope of the collective bargaining relationship. An example of this governmental function occurred when I was chairman of the food industry's labor-management committee. The industry was faced with a serious problem involving considerable litigation because of certain OSHA requirements on the use of personal protective equipment in the retail meat departments of supermarkets. Neither the industry nor the unions had been consulted in the formulation of these regulations, and as a result there was disagreement as to when and how this equipment should be used. OSHA had brought a number of lawsuits to enforce its interpretations. The food industry committee was in a position to obtain union and management agreement on a common understanding of how the regulations should be applied and to present OSHA with a joint position. OSHA cooperated by producing a clarification of the regulations that proved acceptable to the food industry. This process required nearly nine months of consultations, but it brought about the withdrawal of costly and time-consuming litigation. I believe the committee is now in a position to continue working closely with OSHA and has perhaps created a model for dealing with other federal regulatory processes to influence either the formulation or application of regulatory policies affecting labor relations.

The model just described is a new way of playing the old

collective bargaining game, but it is not the only one. I have not even touched on the special problems of the public sector, the health industry, and other areas of labor relations where there is much to be done to create or to restore effective collective bargaining. This task cannot be accomplished solely through the efforts of third party neutrals like the Federal Mediation and Conciliation Service. For many years the collective bargaining process engaged the best efforts of many dedicated and talented people whose ideas and energies made the process work. We know that there has never been a time when collective bargaining has not been in some kind of trouble.

It is possible to solve the problems labor leaders and corporate managers face today in collective bargaining through dedication and talent. So I charge the representatives of labor and management, who have the ultimate responsibility to make the system work, to be mindful of the uniquely pragmatic quality of collective bargaining; to keep intact the best of what has been accomplished; to create the innovations necessary to advance the system; and to keep the spirit of the past for the work of the future.

2

Output: Collective Bargaining and Productivity

William W. Winpisinger

Before I directly discuss ways in which collective bargaining affects worker productivity, a few general observations on the American work force, though perhaps not precisely in point, would be appropriate as a frame of reference.

Contrary to impressions created by the media and in particular by the Department of Health, Education, and Welfare's now famous report, *Work in America*, American workers, taken as a whole, are not disgruntled, dissatisfied, disaffected, or alienated from their jobs or from the nation's economic system. One beneficial result of the HEW study was that it generated subsequent investigations analyzing in depth the fundamental issue of job satisfaction. By asking the right questions, social scientists have discovered what most union representatives somehow already knew deep down in their gut. While every worker wants to improve his wages, hours, and working conditions, the vast majority of workers are not as alienated by their jobs as the HEW report would have us believe. In fact most of the subsequent studies have shown that 85 percent of the nation's workers generally express sentiments about their jobs that range from mere contentment to sheer pride. This includes those who go into the nation's factories and workshops to perform the hard, dirty, and often hazardous jobs that are the foundation of our industrialized society.

I am stressing this point at the outset because I am disturbed by those in the media and elsewhere who attempt to portray American workers as somehow less motivated, and thus less productive, than their counterparts in such places as Germany, Sweden, or Japan. As part of the Machinists Union's relationship with the International Metalworkers Federation, the International Transport Workers Federation, and other organizations representing the world labor movement, we are in frequent contact with visiting delegations of foreign trade unionists. When these brothers and sisters from other countries travel in the United States—visiting factories, maintenance depots, repair facilities, construction sites, and other work places—they are generally surprised at how hard Americans work. More than one of my union colleagues from overseas has asked me why Americans feel they have to work at such a fast and furious pace. Though it is fashionable to criticize American workmanship, the fact is that most Americans, including union members, are eager to give a good day's work for a good day's pay.

Recent proposals to supplant or supplement collective bargaining with various devices to improve productivity are largely predicated on unfounded notions of worker alienation. Organized labor is opposed to any attempt to diminish the force of the adversary process of collective bargaining, such as the Kelso Plan, codetermination, and the steel industry's Experimental Negotiating Agreement. Employee stock ownership improperly ties the employee's financial interest to the employer's without managerial authority, but with a frequently unreasonable risk of loss. Codetermination generally relegates workers on corporate boards of directors to a subordinate role, vitiates union leadership, and fails to respond to workers' needs. Nor can any third party called upon to resolve a labor-management bargaining impasse adequately assert the interests of union members.

Having unburdened myself of these preliminary observations about the general productivity of the American work force and the state of the collective bargaining art, I am now prepared to set forth evidence of the manner in which collective bargaining has contributed to the doubling of productivity in the last thirty years.

Anyone conversant with the history of working conditions during the course of the industrial revolution realizes that one of the ways in which collective bargaining increased individual productivity was by bringing about a reduction in the length of the work day. During the early years in which our society began to change from an agrarian society to a predominantly industrial one, factory hands were expected to work the same number of daily and weekly hours as farm hands. It took a long time—about 150 years in fact—for management to realize that although the human body could function efficiently from sunup to sundown at the relaxed rhythm of work in the fields, it could not sustain the pace of the factory.

But change did not evolve from recognition of this obvious fact. The twelve-hour day and the seven-day week hung on in some industries—including the basic steel industry—as late as the 1920s. I can remember old-timers in the working class neighborhood in which I grew up who could tell you what it was like to work day after day, week after week, twelve hours a day and seventy-two hours a week. And I am just old enough— or young enough—to know that the eight-hour day, forty-hour week did not just happen. Shorter hours were a product of collective bargaining. And though management generally resisted the idea of paying workers as much for ten hours as for twelve, or for eight hours as for ten, the result has proven that over the long run workers can produce more in five eight-hour days than in six or seven twelve-hour days.

However, we have not had a general reduction in the work week since World War II. Labor has been able to chip away little free time in added holidays and vacations. The reduction of the forty-hour week is long overdue to compensate for increased productivity. The thirty-five hour week will also reduce unemployment and improve the lives of working people.

The direct relationship between productivity and collective bargaining can also be seen in the results from continuing pressure at the collective bargaining table for better wages and other job-related benefits. This may sound paradoxical. How can labor be made more productive by making it more expensive? When labor is cheap, management can afford to squander it without much thought for efficiency. In China and India, for example, earth removal for dams and road building is a matter of assembling thousands of people with baskets on their backs. In this country the work of those thousands of poorly paid people is performed by dozens of well-compensated, properly equipped workmen.

When labor succeeds in putting a premium on itself, management must respond by using it sparingly and efficiently. In a very real sense, then, the development of labor-saving technology has been a direct result of collective bargaining. Because of technology, unit labor costs have gone down, and output per man hour has gone up. The average industrial worker produces more than twice as much today as he did at the end of World War II. In industry after industry (including such basic industries as auto, steel, rubber, and aerospace), more goods are produced by fewer workers. Organized labor does not oppose automation or computerization. It recognizes that higher standards of living are tied to ever increasing productivity.

Not only the absolute level of wages, but also the relative earning power of American workers affects individual productivity. While some people may believe labor is over-paid and under-worked, few blue collar workers can provide their families with a "moderate" standard of living as defined by the Department of Labor—a yearly income of $16,000 for a family of four living in an urban area, or an average hourly wage of $8.00. The real wages of American workers have in fact declined, and the distribution of income in the United States has become less equitable during the last decade. In response to double-digit inflation and unfair wage controls, workers are now demanding annual wage increases of about 10 percent plus cost-of-living clauses.

A third way in which collective bargaining affects productivity is by providing an orderly and equitable procedure for settling grievances in the work place. Those who deprecate this element of productivity do not know much about human nature or industrial relations. The longer grievances go unsettled, the more production suffers. Most companies with any experience and sophistication in industrial relations are well aware of this and are accordingly willing to let stewards leave their work stations when grievances arise. They know that when a grievance is settled, it benefits not just the worker or the union, but the company as well.

Another way in which collective bargaining affects the overall productivity of the American work force is through negotiations aimed at reducing the incredible toll of industrial accidents and diseases. By now, people with even superficial or indirect knowledge of industrial employment know that working in a mill, mine, factory, or foundry is highly hazardous to human health. The U.S. Department of Labor estimates that at least twenty-five million accidents each year are serious enough to cause some disability and loss of working time. At least 25,000 workers are killed on the job annually and another 100,000 die from long-term exposure to asbestos, beryllium, carbon monoxide, industrial solvents, vinyl chloride, and many of the other 50,000 chemicals used in modern production. As in the case of kepone, the effect of many chemicals is not known until it is too late. In addition, every working day as many as seventeen million Americans are exposed to noise levels that cause impaired hearing, high blood pressure, heart attacks, and psychological disorders.

The resulting loss in terms of production may not be measurable, but it cannot be disputed. Every time a worker is hospitalized or bedridden or buried as the result of a job-related accident or occupational disease, the nation's productive capacity suffers. One of the very direct ways in which unions try to limit this loss is by negotiating for plant safety committees, which are encouraged to work with management as well as with state and federal agencies to reduce safety and health hazards in the work place. To the extent that collective bargaining is a mechanism for reducing the physical and psychological dangers of industrial employment, it serves as a catalyst for increased production.

Still another way in which collective bargaining affects worker productivity is by encouraging the establishment of apprentice training programs. Even in the midst of recent periods of high unemployment, skilled journeymen, and especially machinists and other skilled metal workers, have been in demand. In many cities there just are not enough to go around. The shortage of trained craftsmen in metalworking industries has increased ever since the end of World War II. For generations the railroads were the primary source of such workers, but the postwar decline in the railroad industry brought about an equivalent decline in the number of metalworking apprenticeships.

As a union, we are concerned about the lack of apprentice training opportunities in the United States. Our representatives are directed, as a matter of union policy, to try to negotiate apprenticeship clauses in every new contract. Unfortunately, we have had limited success in convincing employers that this kind of training will pay off in increased productivity over the long run. Most employers would rather take their chances with journeymen pirated from competitors or from other countries.

Throughout the years, collective bargaining has been constantly adapted to meet changing needs. One problem that has had a definite effect on worker productivity is alcoholism. Many employers tell us that it has become a major personnel problem. According to government estimates, 10 percent of all working-age Americans are alcoholics. Alcoholism reduces the nation's total productive capability by increasing absenteeism, tardiness, and on-the-job accidents. It reduces individual productivity by what many workers call "on-the-job absenteeism": a worker punches in and gets paid even though all he produces is scrap because his hands are shaking and his head is aching from last night's hangover.

I might say, incidentally, that alcoholism is as prevalent in the executive suite as it is on the factory floor, and that all together it costs an estimated fifteen billion dollars a year in direct production losses. In response to this problem, we are working with employers in joint labor-management alcoholism programs. We have drafted contract language for the guidance of our representatives, and some of our programs, especially in the airlines industry, have become models for employers and unions in other industries. Union members who come out of the shop, having experienced the problem first hand, have been successfully trained to serve as alcoholism counselors for their fellow workers. To the extent that the bargaining process helps unions and management agree upon programs to reduce alcoholism in the work force, bargaining contributes to increased productivity in the work place.

In sum, collective bargaining contributes directly to productivity in manifold ways. I believe that a worker produces better when he is fairly compensated for a fair week's work. He produces better when he feels fairly treated, when his work place is safe, when he is provided with better training and better tools to do the job. He produces best, however, when he has a fair stake in the economic system.

Collective bargaining cannot alone assure increasing productivity, but it is necessary for the achievement of any substantial gains. Action must also be taken outside of contract negotiations to assure the productivity of American business and industry and the equitable distribution of its rewards. To maintain the viability of the collective bargaining system, its participants and practitioners must seek to expand the system's dimensions to encompass their burgeoning problems.

Part 2
The Economic Dimension

3

Collective Bargaining and Automation

Theodore W. Kheel

The difficult collective bargaining problems caused by rapid technological change involve the most crucial of the legitimate interests of labor and management. For the employer, automation offers the promise of competitive advantages in terms of higher output and economies of scale and lower labor costs. For the employee, automation represents a threat to job security and, in some instances, to an entire craft or profession.

At the same time, labor and management share interests even in this sensitive area, since business must be competitive to safeguard jobs and unions have an obligation to improve the quality of work their members perform. The adversary bargaining process is capable of resolving technological conflicts in labor relations. This was dramatically demonstrated by events surrounding the 1963 New York City newspaper strike, as reported in an extraordinary three-page account by A. H. Raskin in *The New York Times* following the strike. The purpose of this chapter is to describe the continuing effects of automation on collective bargaining in the newspaper industry as an example of the systemic significance of automation, based on my experience as the industry's mediator.

The *Times* article was a classic report of a labor dispute. Raskin got into the guts of the dispute and the bargaining process, analyzing the specifics of what had happened during the 114-day strike rather than employing the more frequent journalistic treatment of reporting just the results: the agreement reached, how much was agreed to, the other terms, the parties' mutual congratulations, and so forth. I did not fully appreciate it at the time, but the 1963 contract represented not only the culmination of tough negotiations, but the beginning of a complex new process. It amounted to an eleven-year mediation—the most extended bargaining in which I have participated—and resulted in the historic agreement of 1974.

In the course of those eleven years, many changes occurred in the milieu in which the bargaining took place, the newspaper industry conducted its business, and the city of New York existed. For example, the composition and concentration of the city's population changed, thus altering the nature of the demand for publications. The technology of print communications also changed. Television became a stronger competitor. As a result, different types of publications sprang into existence. In the island of Manhattan, demand for the "newspaper of record," *The New York Times,* declined; the demand for the paper in the suburbs began to increase. But the mechanics of covering the news in the suburbs, of appealing to suburban readership in competition with suburban newspapers, presented new problems.

In 1963, when I became involved at the request of Mayor Wagner, the New York City newspaper industry consisted of thirteen newspapers. We now have three. Collective bargaining has often been blamed for the demise of the other ten. In retrospect we would more properly say that the other ten were doomed to fail anyway because of external forces, and that collective bargaining mainly affected the date of their inevitable fate. In practically every city throughout the country, the number of newspapers has declined, primarily because of competition with electronic media. It has happened in London as well as in New York, and in San Francisco, Los Angeles, Philadelphia, and Chicago. But perhaps the most important change in the bargaining setting has been technological in nature, and it has had a tremendous impact on employer-employee relationships in the newspaper industry.

Each newspaper consists of three businesses: the business of writing articles, the business of printing what is written, and the business of distributing what is printed. Most other publications, like magazines, are engaged in only one business, the writing business. They contract out printing and distribution. The newspapers perform all three operations in sequence: writing, printing, and distribution. They employ members of ten different unions during different times of the day under different working conditions requiring different skills. The unions all bargain with the same employer under the same general economic and social conditions, and they look to the wages and benefits the other unions have achieved when formulating their own demands—a phenomenon not confined to the unions of the newspaper industry and generally known as "me tooism."

The specific technological developments that occurred in newspaper publishing came to bear initially and primarily, though not exclusively, on the printing unions. New typesetting technology affected particularly the printers working in the composing room where the paper is "made up" into pages. The change in technology was not confined to the printing function of the composing room; it also affected related business functions—billing, accounting, and record keeping. The new typesetting methods were not only used in the composing room, where type has traditionally been set, but also in the classified ad department, where advertising copy is taken over the telephone, the advertiser's credit is checked, and his bill is prepared and sent to him. The new technology consolidated many functions and permitted greater efficiency. But it did more than merely make the wheel turn faster; it permitted the publisher to reduce the size of the work force and to lower the level of skill required to compose the paper.

The skills employed in the composing room remained substantially the same for sixty years after *The New York Sun* settled a three-year strike over the introduction of typesetting machinery in 1903. At that time, typesetting by hand was mechanized through the introduction of Linotype, the trade name of the first machine to radically change the composition process. From 1903 on, certain skills were required of those who did the composing work. It took five years of apprenticeship to become a journeyman. Some say it could have been learned in less time, but it was not a simple skill.

Modern typesetting equipment is remarkable in that it can be operated in large part by anyone who can learn to type. Not take shorthand—just type. As a result, a young girl right out of high school can perform almost as well as a seasoned compositor who has been around for thirty or forty years. In fact, many of the old-timers whose fingers had gotten mashed a few times in the composing room could operate a large Linotype keyboard, but had trouble hitting one key at a time on the new typewriter-size keyboards. Operating a keyboard is the sum total of the work now required to make up a paper. The new equipment does most of the rest by itself, and every day there are further technological advances. I cannot think of anywhere in our society where automation has provoked as sudden or as far-reaching a revolution in the way work is done as in the newspaper industry.

The initial reaction of the printers' union was total hostility. Like the nineteenth century Luddites, the union wanted to stop the machine to preserve its jobs. It succeeded in doing so temporarily, ironically to the temporary advantage of the newspapers. After the fact—that is after the 1963 contract—the newspapers discovered that the technology had changed so fast that, but for the union's obstinate opposition, they would probably have bought a lot of machines and trained a lot of people in typesetting techniques that quickly became obsolete. Capital expenditures would have been lost and the process of bargaining with the union and training its members would have had to be repeated until the technology became more stable.

By 1974, a tremendous change had taken place in the thinking of the members of the Typographical Union and their president, Bertram Powers. As a consummate union politician, Powers was not about to put himself in the dangerous position of leading his members without their support. When the leadership becomes, in Whitney Young's phrase, a "follow-ship," a union leader is in danger of losing his pants. When it came to union politics, Bert Powers wore both a belt and suspenders. He knew he had to educate his members to obtain their support in saving their own jobs, and he knew he could not move any faster than their ability to understand what was happening. But union members were in no mood to listen in the early 1960s when new technology was entering the printing industry, first in job printing (of books, catalogues, and the like) and then in newspapers. Members of the New York printers' union began to lose jobs to other cities and to non-union shops using newer equipment. The pressure on the union to accept automation mounted.

The first occasion on which the Typographical Union endorsed the new technology was, I believe, at McGraw-Hill, around 1970. McGraw-Hill publications, which include some twenty-five magazines, had at one time been written, printed, and distributed in New York City. The printing left New York City when McGraw-Hill discovered that it did not pay to ship paper from New York City to Chicago and California and other places where its magazines were sold. For national publications, it made economic sense to print in a central location, like Chicago, or in several places around the country. The new technology permitted the publisher to make up the magazine in New York and then send the copy by plane to any place where it made sense to do the press work.

With the press work went the composition. But McGraw-Hill discovered over the years that there were disadvantages in doing the composition out of town. The writers were in New York City and they were not about to move to Kalamazoo. After the stories were written, the writers had to get proofs to make changes and corrections. Then the pages had to be laid out. To facilitate this editorial process, the composing work had to remain for the most part in New York, where it is now done with computers in McGraw-Hill's own office building on 46th Street and Avenue of the Americas. Typesetting can be done at night with proofs completed by the following morning. The composing work for twenty-five magazines is done in a room not much larger than a good-size living room. McGraw-Hill has even gone into the business of composing magazines for other publishers.

When McGraw-Hill recognized the potential value of the new technology, they went to Bert Powers and said, "Will you allow us to use this equipment if we agree to bring this work back to New York?" His choice was, in effect, between zero union members doing composing work or, as it turned out, fifty (as against five hundred that might have been required under the old system). Not being a silly man, he agreed. There are now about one hundred typographers doing this work at McGraw-Hill.

The final newspaper negotiations began when the contract expired in March of 1973. There was by then an eleven-year history behind the automation issue, intertwined with many other bargaining issues, personal factors, and inter-union relationships. The extent to which the other newspaper unions would honor or break the picket line of the printers' union, which had chosen to strike *The New York Times,* was unknown. Every legal strategy and tactic of collective bargaining that companies and unions have developed was utilized, including court injunctions, and a few methods perhaps technically outside the law were used as well. The negotiations, which centered around the automation of composing, were turbulent and prolonged.

A newspaper, insofar as the composing part of the work is concerned, has three main categories of typesetting: classified advertising, display advertising, and editorial content. In the course of the bargaining I was told by the *Times* that classified ads could be automated within thirty days, editorial material within three to five years, and display ads within a somewhat longer time. Detailed proposals about the introduction of new equipment over a period of time in the three composing operations were made, debated, and rejected.

Underlying all of this, of course, were the primary concerns of the newspapers and the unions. The papers insisted on absolute freedom to introduce new technology as they saw fit. The union demanded absolute job security for its members. The papers were eventually willing to guarantee protection against the loss of jobs due to the new technology, but not the loss of jobs due to economic conditions. The papers said: "If our business drops off, we may have to lay off people for that reason. We will not guarantee employment against an economic decline; we will only guarantee it against a decline due to automation." The union said: "How do you know whether the decline is an economic decline or a decline due to the new technology? And besides, if our concern is the protection of jobs, we are not going to give up our lever, which is to prevent you from using the new technology until we get a complete guarantee."

The turning point came in a meeting at my Manhattan apartment. The union proposed a bargain based upon complete acceptance of the demands of both sides: 100 percent job security in return for 100 percent freedom to introduce new technology. After a great deal of soul-searching, the *Times*, the *News*, and the *Post* agreed to guarantee the job of every printer then on the job in return for a completely free hand in automation. The contract involved other major innovations in the bargaining process related to the technological issue, including an eleven-year term, arbitration of economic questions, and the establishment of an early retirement fund. The cost to the papers was high, but the benefits were great.

The effects of the new technology on the printing industry have only just begun. The *Times* has automated its classified ads and is beginning to do the same with display ads and editorial matter. The *News* and the *Post* have less classified advertising and are therefore concentrating on other uses, while papers like the *Los Angeles Times* and the *Miami Herald* have more fully adopted the new technology. Progress is being made in developing new typesetting processes as well. The city's three papers have been able to survive the often difficult conditions for doing business in New York largely as a result of automation.

Collective bargaining has, in the process, successfully resolved problems of the first magnitude for New York City, center of the publishing and communications industries, and for our society. Newspapers are essential to the free exchange of opinion and ideas in our democracy. At the same time, the harmonizing of work relationships and technological progress is no less crucial. The realization of both goals in the great print media is a hopeful harbinger of the future for all working Americans.

4
Collective Bargaining and Inflation

Glenn E. Watts

Since collective bargaining is intimately related to general economic conditions, the abnormal occurrence in recent years of both high inflation and high unemployment, or "stagflation," has resulted in anomalous bargaining conditions and contractual settlements. To illustrate the point, it may be useful to oversimplify: inflation creates pressure for higher wages; unemployment leads to reduced wage demands. What, then, is the effect of stagflation?

General economic conditions tend to have similar effects on all workers and industries, but there are great differences in the cost of living and the unemployment rate between New York City and Des Moines. The United States, nevertheless, has an absolutely intradependent economic system in which events in one area have effects in other areas. Trade deficits, monetary fluctuations, government spending, as well as recessionary and inflationary events all affect collective bargaining on wages. Moreover, wage settlements with major industrial unions and public employee groups have effects on wage settlements in other parts of the collective bargaining system.

The responses of various unions to stagflation have been diverse. The steelworkers have sought a guaranteed annual wage as a way of taking into account both the decline in real income resulting from inflation and the threat to job security resulting from economic stagnation. The auto workers have sought a reduction of the forty-hour work week to thirty-five hours in order to achieve a relative gain in wages while increasing employment opportunities. Recent contracts in the oil, aluminum, and communications industries have all addressed the difficult problems raised by current economic conditions in different ways.

Job security has become an area of overriding concern for unions, but the most intractable of all bargaining problems are those created by inflation and the worker's loss of earning power. Economists may have established theoretical and programmatic notions about controlling unemployment, but they disagree sharply about how best to dampen inflation. Political scientists have few policies to propose, and government has had little experience in managing inflation.

The problems created by inflation are monetary. Inflation has ranged from 5 percent to over 10 percent annually during the 1970s. A dollar increase in the hourly rate won at the bargaining table may be worth only seventy-five cents by the end of a three-year contract. A dollar in pension benefits negotiated in 1970 may literally not be worth a nickel by 1985. Inflation has required drastic increases in employers' contributions to pension funds to ensure American workers a secure retirement.

The consumer price index, with a base figure of 100 for 1967, will nearly double by the end of this decade. What an American worker could buy for $100 in 1967 now costs nearly $180 and, by 1980, will cost almost $200. As I have traveled around the country, I have found great apprehension among our union's members, most of whom are employed, about unemployment. But they are bewildered and many times embittered by inflation.

The social advances that American workers made in the 1950s and 1960s were in large measure the product of wage increases negotiated at the bargaining table. American workers were for the first time able to buy homes and cars, send their children to college, and afford a decent standard of living.

These gains are being eroded by unremitting inflation, and there is rising concern that collective bargaining cannot protect the worker against such losses.

One of the deepest desires of most working men and women, and indeed of the majority of American people, is to own a private home on a small piece of land. The first house I ever bought cost $12,375. Today the same house might cost five, six, or seven times as much. The question must now be asked whether working people can afford their own homes. The answer is that, for most workers, this modest goal has become somehow out of reach. I recently attended a conference where it was stated that the average American must adjust his other expectations to the prospect of owning a condominium. What once was a noble ambition, encouraged by government and other social institutions, including business, has now become unrealistic, even improper.

In fact, the attitude of many business leaders with whom I have had discussions appears to be that high profit margins must be maintained, but that inflation can only be solved by workers absorbing wage reductions.

Instead of workers taking inflation lying down, job dissatisfaction will become more widespread, productivity will fall, and industrial unrest will intensify. Real wage increases are an essential incentive without which work becomes less rewarding. An unhappy employee produces less and is more inclined to strike than one who is satisfied.

Wage demands will continue to mount as long as inflation persists. Cost-of-living adjustment (COLA) clauses must be seen by management as the only way to stabilize the negotiating process and to prevent a wage-price spiral. Without COLA provisions, pressures for higher wages are unrestrained and the limits of the bargaining process break down.

I cannot imagine a union being willing to settle a contract today without a cost-of-living escalator. And if they do settle without a COLA, there must be either a one-year agreement or a provision permitting negotiations on wages to be reopened every year during the term of the contract. Such devices only postpone the task of dealing with inflation and cause disruption in orderly labor relations—a true irony, when a contract exists for the primary purpose of minimizing disputes. In the future, all unions are bound to press demands for wage indexing.

The labor movement must also look to the political system for relief from inflation. For the first time in eight years, both the White House and Congress are controlled by the Democratic party. President Carter is someone union members and businessmen alike can trust to deal with economic issues in an evenhanded manner. Labor does not expect the president to dance to its tune, but it believes its views are entitled to be given appropriate weight in our pluralistic democracy. What the federal government does about the great economic issues will directly affect the collective bargaining process and its results, and I expect the effects to be beneficial to workers.

Tax cuts can increase the net income of workers as much as wage increases. Government benefits are a form of untaxed supplementary income. Both bear on the declining purchasing power of the worker. Where appropriate, the labor movement will lend its support to tax relief and categorical grants.

Not all government appropriations are spent. There is disturbing evidence that many funds never reach their intended beneficiaries. This means that, to some extent, the economic "pump-priming" that government spending is supposed to accomplish does not occur. If government is to play a constructive economic role, it must pursue a demonstrably sound Keynesian program of tax reductions, economic subsidies, and deficit spending to stimulate economic growth.

Not all government spending is inflationary. The emergency housing bill that failed to pass Congress this year would have provided 800,000 construction workers with jobs that generate tax revenues and reduce government spending for unemployment, welfare, and other forms of assistance. The new homes would have increased the supply of housing and reduced the highly inflationary prices of homes.

Labor will also seek public benefits that substitute for wage increases and can have significant anti-inflationary effects. The most notable examples are in health care, where collective bargaining is virtually incapable of keeping pace with rising medical and hospital costs. Government funding of health maintenance organizations would tend to reduce both wage demands and health care costs. A growing emphasis on political remedies to economic problems is one of the larger, long-term effects of inflation on labor relations.

Collective bargaining is an imprecise art. It is difficult to describe the many effects of inflation on its practice, but they are pervasive and potentially destructive. If the fundamental faith of American workers in the fairness of the bargaining process is lost, then we will have to discover other methods for peacefully resolving disputes between labor and management.

Part 3
The Political Dimension

5

Depoliticizing the Bargaining Process

Benjamin F. Bailar

Collective bargaining between the U.S. Postal Service and postal employees faces an uncertain future. This is because the entire concept of the Postal Service is under siege, and one of the most important elements in postal reform is collective bargaining. The organization of the postal system has determined the nature of the bargaining relationship, and the bargaining relationship has been an important factor in the reorganization of the postal system. The history of this extraordinary interaction and its future direction are the subject of this chapter.

The Postal Reorganization Act of 1970 was the keystone of a new era of labor-management relations in the postal service. Prior to 1970, the Post Office was a political department of the federal government headed by the cabinet-level Postmaster General, and wages were determined by congressional action. As a result of the Act, the Postal Service was established as a public corporation beyond direct political control, with wages determined by collective bargaining. There is now some support, however, for returning the postal service to direct political control. While some postal unions may believe a reversion to political control would be in their interest, I do not believe the termination of collective bargaining would benefit the public, the postal system, or postal employees. The political system would not have accomplished for Postal

Service employees what has been accomplished under collective bargaining in the last few years, nor could we expect the stable, productive, labor-management relations recently experienced to continue under a political regime.

Prior to reorganization, the Postal Service was the political trading block of the federal government. People bought jobs, contracts were awarded because of influence, and the postal system was managed according to the dictates of the political system. The management of the Postal Service is now based on private sector concepts and techniques, including efforts to advance career postal employees on the basis of merit, to train employees for better jobs, and to resolve labor-management disputes through either collective bargaining or arbitration. To be fair, it is possible that the current progress of the postal system might continue under a political system. But in my judgment, those who argue that is likely to happen have not learned the lessons of the history of collective bargaining with the postal system.

The relationship between the Postal Service and its unions dates from 1889, when postal unions were formed (long before many private sector unions). Their original purpose was to represent the interest of the postal workers in the political process. Instead of negotiating the bread-and-butter issues, they pursued their goals through legislative lobbying. This resulted in legislation that provided pay increases, limited hours of work, and fixed working conditions. Eventually the postal unions gained a great deal of influence on Capitol Hill; influence they still enjoy.

The Kennedy administration formalized labor-management relations in the federal government by an executive order that permitted representation elections for federal employees and provided a framework for labor-management relations. However inadequate, this was a step forward. During the Nixon administration federal labor relations were further advanced by executive order. These steps were welcome, but they were insufficient to meet mounting pressures generated by the problems of the Postal Service. The Kappel Commission was established by President Johnson to study the specific problems of the Post Office Department after a serious breakdown in the mail system brought the Chicago Post Office to a halt in the mid-sixties. In 1969 the Commission reported, "few things in our study have so disturbed us as learning of the severely limited career opportunities of postal employees and the physical working conditions and institutional environment in which they work."

By 1970, 69 percent of the buildings of the Postal System were outmoded or obsolete; 80 percent of the employees were in facilities designed for a time when mail volume was less than half its current volume; 80 percent of all postal employees leaving the department did so at the same level they were hired, and the postal pay scale lagged behind private industry. I cannot think of a less challenging, less stimulating, less rewarding atmosphere in which to work.

Based on the recommendations of the Kappel Commission, the White House sent a postal reform bill to Congress in 1969, establishing the Postal Service as a government corporation. The postal unions and others opposed that legislation. It was not until the spring of 1970, following a one-week work stoppage involving about 200,000 postal employees, that the Postal Reorganization Act became a politically viable proposal. To bring an end to the work stoppage, the administration reached an agreement with the unions that provided for a 6 percent pay raise retroactive to December 1969. The unions agreed to support the Postal Reform Act, providing there were certain modifications to the corporate concept. The final legislation retained the basic thrust of turning the political Post Office into the businesslike Postal Service, including broad rights to collective bargaining as experienced in the private sector in return for substantial concessions to the postal union. The Reorganization Act included an additional 8 percent pay raise upon passage of the law, and a provision for negotiating a compression agreement which would reduce from twenty to eight the number of years necessary for an employee to reach the maximum in his or her pay grade. The Postal Reorganization Act of 1970 was a demonstration of the political power of the postal unions and how they could achieve labor relations goals outside collective bargaining.

The most significant provisions of the Postal Reorganization Act concerned labor-management relations, which became generally subject to the National Labor Relations Act. Like most private employers, postal management had to sit down and bargain collectively with the postal unions on wages, hours, and working conditions. Unlike private sector workers, postal employees were not given the right to strike. Instead, a dispute-settling mechanism was initiated that included fact-finding and culminated in binding third-party arbitration. In addition, the Act set forth certain principles of compensation and benefit levels for all postal employees, continued the participation of postal employees in the Federal Civil Service Retirement Program, and granted postal unions benefits then available to all other federal employees.

Another important difference between postal employees and private sector employees is that the Reorganization Act made certain provisions for the benefit of so-called management organizations that seek to gain the benefits of organized labor while retaining the prerogatives of management. As may be imagined, this represents a continuing major problem for the Postal Service. It results in more frequent lawsuits between the Postal Service and the management organizations than between the Postal Service and the unions. Finally, the Reorganization Act continued the application of a variety of statutes limiting management's ability to control and to develop personnel policies with complete freedom. These statutes do not, of course, apply to the private sector. The postal unions were newly merged with the differing views of inter-union jurisdictions and the widely varying aspirations of employees in 32,000 postal facilities ranging from big industrial centers to the smallest of hamlets.

As a result of reorganization, the Postal Service does not have a traditional private sector collective bargaining relationship with its employees despite the popular impression to the contrary. The collective bargaining process in the Postal Service is actually a hybrid, combining some of the features of federal labor relations with some of the features of private sector collective bargaining. This hybrid has demonstrated remarkable vigor in successfully coping with the problems of Postal Service employees and management.

The first postal service collective bargaining agreement went into effect on July 21, 1971. It was a major agreement, freely reached by the designated representative of the employees and the management of a federal agency. When the parties first sat down together in the spring of 1971, there were feelings of apprehension and of hope on both sides. Union representatives and mangement were faced with a whole gamut of salary and benefit issues, with the union seeking higher pay scales from an employer newly responsible for controlling its costs. Both parties knew that out of political necessity they were expected to reach an early agreement without the outside aids provided for in the Reorganization Act. I think it is a tribute to the system the Act established that they were able to achieve an agreement with only one fact-finding proceeding and with no work stoppage. We have since negotiated two more agreements, in the summer of 1973 and in the summer of 1975, without disruption in the work force and without third-party participation.

These three contracts represent numerous accomplishments by the Postal Service and its employees and the correction of many of the injustices that concerned the Kappel Commission. The average postal employee now earns more than $17,000 a year including fringe benefits. After spending $2 billion on construction and modernization, 99 percent of postal employees work in new or improved facilities. Excellent employee and management training programs have been established. As a result of the merit promotion system, there is no limit to the job aspirations of a postal employee. A man who started twenty-seven years ago as a substitute letter-carrier was recently appointed a regional postmaster general in the western United States, a job that involves managing a work force of about 150,000 people.

The concerns of employees and management have shaped the present national collective bargaining agreement, which treats not only matters of wages and hours but also myriad working conditions and other matters of concern to the postal unions.

More important than the terms of the contract, we have found a means to resolve many difficult issues that concern American business and labor, without interference from outside parties. Each agreement to date has included a no layoff clause, for which the Postal Service has been heavily criticized. But job security has probably become the number one issue in every major collective bargaining relationship in the country, and is thereby a source of fundamental labor relations stability. The Postal Reorganization Act prohibited employees from striking against the Postal Service and retained the federal statute that makes striking against the government a felony; the no layoff clause was viewed as a *quid pro quo* for the limitation of the economic weapons of postal employees.

The collective bargaining process has permitted the Postal Service to make progress toward the chief management goal— improved productivity—without laying off a single employee. By reducing the postal work force by 55,000 positions in the last two years through attrition, modernization of facilities, and other methods, the Postal Service has greatly improved its financial status. There was early agreement between postal management and the unions that in order for the Postal Service to provide the American people with the service they expected at a cost they could afford, it was going to be necessary to improve productivity and to increase mechanization. The unions agreed to allow management to introduce mechanization subject to certain procedural restrictions and prohibitions.

Productivity is now the highest it has been in postal history, and American postal productivity is by far the highest of any country in the world.

There is one other aspect of the collective bargaining process in the Postal Service that I think is worthy of note: the arbitration of grievance disputes. In 1973 we took a major step forward and created a system of expedited arbitration. It is still in its infancy, but it has worked well throughout the country. In less than three years, we have had some 4,600 cases filed, resulting in 1,800 decisions rendered by 165 arbitrators from 31 panels administered by the Federal Mediation and Conciliation Service and by the American Arbitration Association. The remaining cases were resolved by the parties before the hearing. In other words, almost 5,000 cases were disposed of in less than three years. This is an especially noteworthy record in view of the fact that this system was created in 1973 and was not fully functional until 1975. The Postal Service's experience with expedited arbitration should encourage its use in the private sector as the only method capable of disposing of the ever rising number of cases under today's collective bargaining agreements.

When the Postal Service was established there were many skeptics who wondered how well it would function and whether the postal unions and the Postal Service were capable of managing their own affairs. Other observers saw the Postal Service as an experiment that might lead to collective bargaining for more federal employees. On the basis of our experience, I am convinced that the Postal Service experiment in collective bargaining has worked well. The Postal Service has lived with the constraints of a hybrid labor-management relationship. The tangible results of collective bargaining have, in my judgment, exceeded the early expectations of both parties and of the public. That is not to say that the relationship between the Postal Service and the postal unions is perfect. Difficult problems and disagreements remain to be resolved. But in the collective bargaining process there is a fair and effective mechanism for finding the solutions.

Yet for all that has been accomplished, some postal unions have now joined those who support the move to return the Postal Service to the political system. We must ask those who advocate undoing postal reform whether a return to political control is in the best interest of the mail system, of the public, or even of the unions. What would be the effect on the collective bargaining relationship?

There is no way, in my opinion, that the Postal Service can be returned to political control without resubmitting the collective bargaining relationship to that same control. The mails are a labor-intensive business. Salaries and benefits make up 85 percent of our costs; the biweekly payroll is $400 million. If management's right to control costs and seek revenue is limited, then management's ability to bargain collectively must be limited. If tied to the political administration, both parties could not be sure that the economic package negotiated at the bargaining table through the free forces of give and take, accomodation, and adjustment—which are the essence of good-faith collective bargaining—would not be subject to revision by the prevailing political forces. Political review of the labor contract, together with political control of postal rates and services, would effectively eliminate true collective bargaining. If the establishment of the Postal Service represented a hopeful step forward for public sector collective bargaining, returning the postal system to political control would be a large step backward and would severely reduce the chances for improvement of collective bargaining elsewhere in the public sector.

Those concerned about nurturing the process of collective bargaining and encouraging its propagation in the public sector should remember that the Postal Reorganization Act was born of labor's strife. Two years ago, one of my first public duties as Postmaster General was to dedicate the stamp proposed by Theodore Kheel and the Institute of Collective Bargaining that melded opposing arrows into a unified design and bore the inscription "Out of Conflict—Accord."

The Postal Service's collective bargaining process is itself the accord that grew out of the 1970 work stoppage. I would not want to see that accord undone. Any major change in the Reorganization Act would obviously affect the collective bargaining process and the future progress of the Postal Service. I think we would have to wait no longer than the summer of 1978, when we negotiate another collective bargaining agreement, to see the difference between collective and political bargaining processes.

Out of the Postal Reorganization Act sprang a labor-management relationship that was perhaps adolescent. It has since progressed rapidly into young adulthood with all the problems associated with personal responsibility. Politicizing the Postal Service would prevent the development of a fully mature collective bargaining relationship. Such regression would only impede progress in the major areas of labor relations while creating new doubts, new fears, new political pressures, and new operating problems. The success of collective bargaining in the Postal Service is an excellent example of the basic soundness of the concept of the Postal Reorganization Act. It has served the interests of labor, management, and ultimately the American people very well. Neither labor unions nor management nor the American people would be well served by the demise of collective bargaining in the Postal Service.

6
Repoliticizing the
Bargaining Process

Albert Shanker

The relationship between politics and public employee collective bargaining is a large subject, and I intend to define it more narrowly in terms of the historical ebb and flow of political tides in the affairs of the United Federation of Teachers. Each of the major public employee unions has evolved in its own way, according to the special circumstances of its members' roles in municipal service and their status in the political community. I would like to relate some of the most significant political events in the growth of teacher collective bargaining in New York City.

The teachers' union was formed in 1916 by leaders of the progressive education movement, whose illustrious numbers included John Dewey and George Counts. They did not foresee a time when teachers would engage in collective bargaining. They believed that teachers, who taught the children of workers, should be in a union because through taking part in the struggles of the parents they could become close to their students and be more successful as teachers. The organization of teachers was initially the result of a social movement guided by an educational philosophy, not of a trade union movement based upon economic demands. Later, during the 1920s and 1930s, the teachers' union became increasingly concerned with political philosophy and was often embroiled in ideological disputes, leading to a split between Communist and non-

Communist groups. It was not until the late 1950s and early 1960s that teachers turned their attention to the nonphilo- sophical tasks of collective bargaining.

Until the era of public employee collective bargaining began, teachers and other municipal employee groups operated largely as political lobbies. They employed political tactics to pursue favorable legislation on wages, hours, and working conditions—the subjects of the collective bargaining process today. Interestingly, the constitutions of the Teachers' Union of the City of New York, the original teachers' union, and of the group that split off from it in the Communism dispute, the Teachers' Guild of New York, gave two highest- ranking union officers the right to enunciate policy, to speak for the organization, and to sign documents. They were the union's president and its legislative representative. The major annual event was the membership's trip to Albany, where they lobbied during each legislative session to increase state aid to education, to prevent cutbacks, or to support one bill or another. In fact, the legislative representative was the *de facto* leader in both the Teachers' Union and the Teachers' Guild, although the president was the *de jure* leader.

When collective bargaining began for teachers, the teacher organizations were still deeply involved in political and social movements unrelated to teachers' working conditions. The Teachers' Union had a great deal of sympathy for and some involvement in Communist causes, while the Teachers' Guild had more of a tendency toward Socialist, Labor, and Liberal Party activity. During the early union election campaigns, it therefore became necessary for the "Young Turks" of the teachers' union movement, like David Selden and myself, to convince old-timers, who were very much involved in political programs, that the movement should be depoliticized. In order to win a majority in a union election and to maintain organizational unity, we needed the support of as many teachers as possible, regardless of their party affiliations or ideological views. Sectarian political issues were of secondary importance to the economic interests all teachers had in common—the bread-and-butter issues.

We believed that some political activity might be possible after representation elections were won, but that depoliticization was a prerequisite of organization. In 1960 the Organizing Committee of the United Federation of Teachers sought the support of teachers for a merger of all teacher organizations. The Organizing Committee was not a union, but a union-in-formation. Teachers were asked to sign a card stating that they would join a union if it could successfully achieve a merger, and they were asked to make a $5.00 down payment toward the annual dues of $18.00. This represented a substantial and somewhat risky commitment since the Teachers' Guild membership—the largest of any teacher group —was then about 2,400 out of a total of some 50,000: only 5 percent membership in an organization in existence for forty-four years, since 1916.

At one point in 1960 the Teachers' Guild considered merging with the Committee for Action through Unity, a group of high school teachers whose 3,000 members had signed pledge cards and had paid $5.00 each. A ratification meeting, held at the old Astor Hotel, was addressed by Michael Quill of the Transport Workers' Union on the values of merger and unionism. But the old-timers debated the merger for hours, asking who these 3,000 teachers were and whether they stood for civil liberties and all the other things for which the old-timers had fought since 1916. To some, increasing the membership seemed to be an opportunistic means of destroying the political values of teacher organizations.

In the meetings of the executive board and the delegate assembly over a period of two or three years in the early 1960s, division between the Young Turks and the old-timers continued and became bitter. The new leaders did not necessarily disagree with the political values and positions of the former leadership, but they argued that higher salaries, better working conditions, and other common concerns were less important than various divisive issues such as the proper interpretation of the First Amendment to the Constitution. In arguing that the union should be depoliticized, the Young Turks compared the union, somewhat ironically, to the candidate for public office who tries to appeal to all voters without alienating anyone, stressing issues that unify rather than divide, and stroking hands and kissing babies.

The teachers' union was at first a political group; it did not become a collective bargaining representative until the 1960s. In 1960 and 1961 there were strikes and referenda, and in 1962 the first contract was negotiated. Of course we retained our legislative representatives in Albany, trying to obtain pension improvements and fighting political skirmishes that arose because of collective bargaining and that undermined the bargaining process. Soon after our first contract, a bill was passed that permitted individual teachers to choose not to be represented by the delegate of the elected bargaining agent, but by the person of his or her choice. This allowed the survival of minority organizations that had lost in the bargaining elections. Thus, the teachers' union discovered it was still inexorably involved in the political system.

By 1968, the teachers' union had negotiated four contracts—in 1962, 1963, 1965, and 1967—and had experienced strikes and all of the manifold difficulties and rewards of collective bargaining. In 1968 I led the union in the three lengthy city-wide strikes over a dispute in the Ocean Hill–Brownsville school district. These strikes were strongly supported by our members and were successfully concluded. It would be fair to say that my stock in trade among the membership was then at a high point. With the initial organizational problems of the union resolved and the organization firmly established, I felt it was appropriate for the teachers' union to enter, or reenter, the political arena.

When I addressed a meeting of our union delegates and chapter chairmen (or shop stewards), I wore a Hubert Humphrey button and, as the last order of business, proposed that the teachers endorse Humphrey for president. I was somewhat surprised when my comments were loudly booed. The specific membership response was that we were a trade union and our job was simply to negotiate salaries and working conditions. I was cautioned that involvement in politics and support for candidates would tend to commit the union's leadership to them, which could be detrimental to the members' interests if other candidates were elected and had responsibility for questions affecting the union. With such a fearful vision of elective politics, there was no endorsement of any candidate in 1968 by either national teacher organization or by New York city and state organizations.

First a political group and then a depoliticized labor union, teachers became *repoliticized* during the late 1960s. The cause of this reversal was not the war in Vietnam or other national political issues of the period, but decentralization of the New York City public schools. Teachers had opposed decentralization, but when it became a reality there were thirty-two school boards to be elected. These boards had certain powers in hiring and firing teachers, allocating and distributing funds, and selecting community school superintendents. Decentralization gave teachers a greater awareness that their job interests were related to the political system, at least on the local district level where contractual rights had to be protected. It became incumbent on teachers either to elect friendly school board members or to defeat unfriendly ones.

The teachers' union has rapidly attained a significant position among potentially political organizations. We have collected large sums of money, but unlike some public employee unions, we have generally not contributed money directly to politicians. We have tried to use our financial resources to activate our membership by developing telephone banks and a political cadre. We pay some of our most active members the same salary to participate in union political activities that they would earn from an after-school job. They in turn recruit volunteers. There were over 2,000 volunteers in the 1976 political campaign, who we helped with babysitters, parking fees, and other expenses. We seek to instill a spirit of camaraderie among volunteers, and there are now thousands who actively participate in the political process through the teachers' union.

The renewed political awareness of teachers was essential in achieving one of the great political events in the history of public employee collective bargaining: the merger of the state teacher association and the state union. While merger at the city level required depoliticization, at least in ideological terms, merger at the state level required repoliticization and the realization that state-wide unity was necessary to affect the state government. For the most part, unions in New York are either New York City–wide unions or New York State–wide unions. One union, the Civil Service Employees Association, is organized state-wide exclusive of New York City. When the majorities of both houses of the state legislature are Republican, which has been the case frequently, the city-wide unions obviously have little access unless they play Republican politics, which few of them do. When control of the legislature is divided, as is the case now, city-wide unions may fare somewhat better, but most bills they sponsor will die as one-house bills. Since the Democrats have controlled both the Senate and the Assembly only once in recent years, state-wide unity is crucial to an effective legislative role.

The state-wide alliance of teachers has already proved to be politically fruitful. Upstate teachers were able to win passage of a pension bill in a year when New York was supposedly in poor financial straits. Without the effective pressure of New York City teachers, there would have been little hope for the Stavisky-Goodman bill requiring educational cutbacks in the city to be no greater than the proportion of all educational spending to the total city budget. The passage of these two bills required mutual concern for the separate but related interests of upstate and downstate teachers. New York's first state-wide teacher organization has been able to overcome the long-standing distrust between city and upstate teachers.

The prospects for achieving similar results through a nation-wide merger of teacher unions are promising. The merger of the 1.5 million-member National Education Association and the .5 million-member American Federation of Teachers may occur in the next few years. Teachers' organizations have already cooperated on national legislative matters and have asserted themselves in the national electoral process. There are teachers in every election district in the country.

New York teachers have given crucial support to state-wide candidates, and their support for President Carter, who needed New York to gain an electoral majority, may have been decisive. This claim is most persuasive in terms of the teachers' major role in nominating Daniel P. Moynihan (who outpolled Carter) instead of Bella Abzug for U.S. Senate. Had Abzug been on Carter's ticket, he may well have lost the state and the presidency.

There are at least two theories about the best way to politically organize all American teachers. The American Federation of State, County, and Municipal Employees and the National Education Association have formed the national Coalition of American Public Employees (CAPE). I have opposed the establishment of a national organization that represents only public employees, and the American Federation of Teachers has refrained from joining CAPE. I fear that the public will see such an organization, which could elect or otherwise determine the officials with whom it would bargain, as a threat to proper labor-management relations and an inevitable threat to democratic government representing all interests.

A political organization of fourteen million public employees, including three million teachers, contains the seeds of its own destruction. In my opinion, the founders of CAPE are inviting repressive legislation like the Hatch Act, which forbids federal employees from engaging in political activities. Instead, public employees should ally themselves with the broader program and larger constituency of the AFL-CIO and the labor movement generally.

"Keep education out of politics and politics out of education" has been a popular rallying cry. Of course, when it comes to public employees and public institutions there has always been politics because such groups are supported by tax revenues and because government funds are allocated through the political process. But before collective bargaining, the political dimension of public employee labor relations was hidden. School administrators, a small and insulated group, dominated educational politics, while teachers were divided over ideological conflicts. These events have been characteristic of teachers' unions across the country. We have witnessed the parallel decline of powerful administrative organizations like the New York Educational Conference Board and the ascendancy of politically mobilized and skillful teachers' unions.

Decentralization was the catalyst for the repoliticization of New York City teachers. Anti-education and anti-public employee union proposals are multiplying rapidly in this era of high taxes and low earnings. I believe such demands will further encourage teachers to assert themselves politically. Only half the states permit collective bargaining by teachers, making the state political process the sole avenue for achieving economic justice for many teachers.

But teachers are increasingly conscious that collective bargaining gains can be lost by national politics that affect aid to education and other aid to the states, by inflationary policies that cheapen wage increases, and by health policies that limit disposable income. Hence collective bargaining is becoming increasingly sensitive to the national political process, not only for teachers but also for auto workers (whose most important bargaining position may be at the side of the car manufacturers lobbying for higher tariffs) and all other American workers.

The teachers' union—first a political organization, then a depoliticized union—may now be said to have entered a third phase as a repoliticized union. The thorough politicization of collective bargaining in New York City's educational institutions has prompted a return, if not to ideological analysis, to a concentration of efforts on intensive lobbying. When the New York City fiscal crisis hit in 1975, contract negotiations began to be overshadowed by the deliberations of the city's Emergency Financial Control Board (the EFCB, dominated by the governor and the mayor). EFCB decisions on teacher salaries and the like rested on political factors largely beyond their control: the federal financing of the city's loans, the federalization of local welfare costs, and the adoption of national health insurance to reduce the cost of municipal hospitals.

Repoliticizing the bargaining process may well lead to the demise of collective bargaining in the public sector. At this time, the American Federation of Teachers represents nearly 15,000 teachers in the State University of New York. The bargaining representative of the state has the permanent option of bargaining to impasse so that the issues on the table may be decided by the state legislature without teachers having recourse to a strike or to a third-party determination of the issues. This means that bargaining on the state level is subject to political review similar to the review of city contracts by the EFCB.

Bargaining by most federal employees, for whom a strike is a crime, is still further from the organizational model of traditional collective bargaining. There is now a critical tension between the political forces exerted by persons external to the bargaining process and the process itself, which may yet reshape public employee labor relations and the political system at large. There are high stakes at risk in this political game, and none of the players can really afford to lose.

Part 4
The International Dimension

7
Bargaining in the World Marketplace

Sol C. Chaikin

Ours is a unique industry. The highly competitive, fluid conditions that prevail in the ladies' garment industry make it particularly sensitive to recessionary and other economic pressures. The essence of ladies' garments is fashion, which fluctuates with as little predictability and with as devastating an effect as demand in any major industry. The sensitivity of the garment industry to recent economic trends (most notably the internationalization of competition in domestic markets) demonstrates certain destructive effects on the structure of collective bargaining—effects that may soon be more widely visible.

The first trend the International Ladies' Garment Workers' Union (the ILGWU) has recently discovered is a geographic redistribution of plants, similar to the long-term movement of other industries out of other northeastern cities, but more limited to New York and more sudden. Formerly the great majority of ladies' dresses were made in and around metropolitan New York, but in the last twenty years there has been a dispersion of the industry to outlying areas in New England; to Virginia and the southern states; and to Pennsylvania, Ohio, and Illinois. The same dispersion has occurred in ladies' sportswear, in lingerie, and in children's dresses. Workers in these relatively new areas have been largely unorganized and the nonunion competition was beginning to threaten union shops in New York City.

We thus determined to do everything possible to maintain the market position of the employers in the greater metropolitan area who bear a heavy competitive burden, particularly those who operate older, less efficient plants. This is not because we chose to favor some employers over others—they all have a right to compete fairly and to be profitable—but the very nature of the industry obliged the union to help maintain a viable manufacturing component and a strong union organization in the New York area.

There is really very little continuity in the production process so far as the end product is concerned, except in the generic sense that all of the products are dresses, blouses, or whatever. We may speak in terms of a lady's dress, but those of you who have had experience as dress-wearers or lady-watchers will know that there are myriad types of ladies' dresses. Many years ago when fashion was otherwise, sportswear was presumed to be used for active sports—like a tennis dress, for example. But these days almost anything may be an item of ladies' sportswear, whether it is to be worn by a participant in the sport, or by a spectator, or for casual occasions in general. The same is true of many articles of women's clothing. The ladies' garment industry produces a wide variety of products at any given time, and its products change rapidly from year to year.

Late in 1975 my colleagues and I took stock of our circumstances as we approached the beginning of negotiations in our major industries on the ladies' dress agreement, the ladies' sportswear agreement, and the children's dress agreement. Three recent developments in the industry became apparent to us at that time, not as separate events just noticed, but as a confluence of destructive developments: 1) the geographic dispersion of low-wage, nonunion shops domestically; 2) the proliferation of contracting-out arrangements among American producers, destabilizing wage rates; and 3) the internationalization of the garment industry with the entry of cheap-labor foreign competitors in the American market. The net effect of these trends was to undermine the organized labor market formerly located in New York City.

The international dimension of collective bargaining in the ladies' garment industry thus converges with domestic factors tending to disperse and to disrupt orderly labor relations. It is the result not of multinationalization of production units, but of even more elemental economic forces. The international dimension of this pattern of events thus exacerbates old domestic difficulties, creates new problems, and multiplies effects that can only be described at some length.

The second trend the ILGWU sees as part of a pattern of events undermining the structure of garment industry collective bargaining concerns the relationship between jobbing-out and garment worker wages. Since we are inherently a piecework and section-work industry, workers theoretically have a financial incentive to produce. Garment workers are not paid an hourly rate with no standard of production; instead, they are paid a dime per unit without a sliding scale based on production levels. The piecework rate has traditionally been a straight-line rate, so that a worker earned a dime for each one of the first fifty or first one hundred units. Average production rates were thought to be determinable based on the experience of employees and employers in a given production setting.

However, the garment industry has been for many years organized on a "jobber" and "contractor" basis. At the beginning of this century whole garments were produced by a single employer who hired and trained employees, obtained raw materials and designs, and produced and marketed the goods. Since then producers have increasingly divorced themselves from production and labor relations because jobbers design the product, contract out its production, then market the finished garment. This represents a degree of production risk-sharing, but a larger motivation is to isolate the labor-intensive production of garments from other components of the industry.

Jobbing-out just does not compare to contracting practices in U.S. heavy industry, such as in the manufacture of cars and machine tools. In most basic industries there are manufacturers and subcontractors who provide certain items. Indeed, some large manufacturers have financed contractors and otherwise encouraged their development. However, an automobile manufacturer who buys wheels from an outside source still brings the wheels to a central assembly plant for final product assembly.

The garment contractor is, in effect, a labor contractor. In one fell swoop he rids himself of the "dirty end of the business"—hiring and firing people, enforcing work standards, dealing with the workers in the day-to-day, face-to-face struggles of the work place. On the other hand, the manufacturer, the "big boss," keeps for himself the "nice end of the business"—hiring the designer, styling the line, and running the showroom with the good-looking models, the well-dressed salesmen, and the buyers from the fancy department stores.

The ILGWU's reaction was to superimpose on this industry practice through collective bargaining a kind of regulatory system based upon the notion that the jobber is the "big boss" responsible for all aspects of the collective bargaining relationship, including wages to be paid by the contractor to the worker, hours of work, and other conditions of employment. Therefore, wages were determined by bargaining between the union and the jobber on the piece rate, using the ultimate selling price of the garment as a factor. In this manner, contractors bidding for the jobber's work would compete not on wage rates, but on delivery and other terms, as well as on the basis of the quality of their work. To prevent "auction block" wages, the ILGWU established a complex system for negotiating the piece rate for each specific garment designed by the jobbers depending upon its selling price and for policing the selling prices of goods subsequently produced by the contractors.

The theory of this system ignored other cost factors affecting the price of the garment. No matter where the contractor's plant was located, the quality of the work done, the amount of employee training, or the level of supervision and management, no matter what type of machines were used or their condition, the piece rate for each like garment was to be the same. In fact, certain standard piece rates were eventually established for certain garment price ranges—for example, $1.25 for sewing an entire dress to be sold at $6.75. If a belt were added to that dress, raising its price without increasing the amount of labor necessary, then the piece rate was automatically increased a fixed amount. When double knit fabrics were introduced, the piece rate jumped because knit cloth was more expensive than a standard wool blend, even though the labor required to sew the former fabric was the same as the latter.

The piece rate bargaining process that had been devised to protect garment workers' wages from predatory competition came to have exactly the effect it was intended to avoid. By failing to take into account productivity-related factors like training and equipment, the ILGWU discouraged modernization by New York manufacturers and encouraged domestic dispersion to low-wage areas and foreign competition. As a result, we have undertaken to negotiate piece rates with the local contractors based upon an analysis of their arm-lengthening devices, equipment attachments, work cycle organization, employee training programs, and other factors that reward employer efficiency and worker productivity. The new wage agreements also provide for the sharing of productivity gains by employer and employees. In addition, we have evolved a guaranteed hourly wage, considerably higher than the federal minimum wage, based on the earnings of a worker of average skill and ability working under average conditions, as defined by industrial engineers in our industry. This higher hourly wage narrows the gap of collective bargaining with contractors and establishes an income floor for garment workers.

Ironically, the new wage structure was first negotiated with employers in outlying areas who resisted the old system of union/jobber–negotiated piece rates. We are now seeking to advance productivity-limited wages and guaranteed earnings in the New York area to assist in the modernization of the American industry, and to contribute to its revival as the leading producer of ladies' garments in the United States and the world. Only by exploiting technological advantages can the future of the labor-intensive New York garment industry's future be vouchsafed.

The third and perhaps most crucial factor in destabilizing labor relations in the garment industry is foreign competition. Fifteen years ago little attention was paid to labels in ladies' and children's apparel. Labels that said "Made in Paris," "Made in France," or "Made in Italy" may have lent status to a garment, but the number of units was small and the prices were high. Foreign competition seemed unthreatening. Who among the United Auto Workers could have guessed that a thousand Rolls Royces, the proverbial cloud no larger than a man's hand, foreshadowed the importation of hundreds of thousands of Volkswagens and Volvos within fifteen or twenty years? During that same period the proportion of ladies' and children's apparel manufactured abroad and sold over the counter in the United States increased from 4 to 25 percent. The leaders of the ILGWU took a good, hard look at these figures and the underlying labor cost statistics and decided the ball game was nearly lost.

A German clothing worker probably earns more than an American ladies' garment worker; the little French seamstress making high fashion clothes as they were made fifty or sixty years ago is not a major threat; nor does Italy produce a large volume of low-cost clothing. But Hong Kong, Taiwan, South Korea, and Thailand have large clothing industries based on cheap labor. Our neighbor Mexico, whose wage rates are incomparably lower than our own, has become a major producer of ladies' apparel, and new sweat-shop garment manufacturers are appearing in the Caribbean.

The competitive advantage of these foreign producers is wholly attributable to their cheap labor supply. The average U.S. garment worker's wage is about $4.25 per hour, with rates in New York somewhat higher and rates in union shops in the southeast somewhat lower. The common wage in Thailand is about $.40 per hour. ILGWU members earn an additional $1.25 per hour in retirement, welfare, and other fringe benefits. American employers must also pay workers' compensation insurance premiums, federal old age benefits, unemployment compensation, taxes, and other costs. The disparity between labor costs here and abroad is tremendous.

But even the most advanced production techniques cannot assure the survival of the American garment industry in face of foreign competition. There are no secrets in our industry. American production techniques and equipment, management science and know-how, even American capital, are exported to countries with one decisive variable in their favor: cheap labor. Half the world's population has an annual income of less than $500. The manufacture of garments requires little initial skill, and the practically limitless supply of labor at subsistance rates could destroy the American garment industry.

American garment workers have generally been drawn from the newest immigrants to this country, and more recently from among Black and Puerto Rican arrivals to northern cities. The entry level jobs that they need to become productive members of society are at stake in the competition between American and foreign clothing manufacturers, and unemployment among garment workers has reached 25 percent in the last few years.

The ILGWU has embarked on a campaign to protect garment workers' wages and jobs. On the political front we have undertaken a massive program to communicate the legitimate concerns of ILGWU members to the American public through broadcast and print advertising. We are also trying to persuade Americans to buy only clothing bearing our union's label. This has been accompanied by intensive efforts to obtain from Congress trade legislation that will provide reasonable protection for American-made clothing in the American market.

On the economic front, the ILGWU has taken the initiative in collective bargaining to reorganize the garment industry. Since there are thousands of small American entrepreneurs operating on narrow profit margins and engaged in the manufacture of ladies' clothing, only the union is capable of performing this stabilizing function. To modernize production techniques the union is hiring industrial engineers for research and development, conducting management programs for contractors, and bargaining for productivity contract clauses.

The destabilization of collective bargaining in the ladies' garment industry is in some part attributable to forces beyond the scope of the bargaining. To a large extent the bargaining process itself must provide a joint labor-management response to the attacks of nonunion domestic manufacturers and cheap-labor foreign producers on the wage structure that supports stable, productive labor relations.

8

Bargaining with the Multinational Corporation

Malcolm L. Denise

The special characteristics of collective bargaining involving multinational companies have been the subject of sharp controversy. During the post–World War II era, I had the opportunity to participate actively in the industrial relations policies of a major multinational corporation (MNC), the Ford Motor Company. My comments generally reflect my own conclusions formed in the course of Ford's experience. Others will have to decide for themselves the extent to which they can accept or generalize from these observations.

Ford's experiences may not be typical of the experience of other MNCs in international labor relations, at least in terms of the length of its experience or the widespread area of its activities today. It has been a multinational firm almost from its inception in 1903, having established its first foreign affiliates by 1908. Today there are Ford affiliates in more than thirty countries around the world.

Both the activities of and the relationships among Ford companies have undergone substantial changes over the years. These changes have been adaptive responses to shifts in economic, market, political, technological, cost, and competitive factors. However, the basic objective of the firm has remained constant: to seek the best ways to sell Ford products in the world's markets for motor vehicles.

The most fundamental conviction to emerge from my

experience is that each country has its own unique institutions, legal system, customs, historical background, attitudes, and expectations—all of which provide the framework for employee-union interactions. This is of key importance. One can try to alter these factors, but one cannot escape the fact that they exist and that they are relevant to what should be undertaken and what can be achieved.

I do not mean to suggest that one should accept the status quo and relax. On the contrary, improvements in practices should be developed. For example, before initiating a change in any one location, management should make a careful analysis of whether a particular practice or policy that has worked well in one place is likely to produce a similar result, or indeed is even feasible, in a second, given the specific institutional factors involved. Failure to make such an analysis carries great risks. An illustration drawn from Ford's experience will amplify this point of view.

An important policy question is whether collective bargaining should be conducted on an individual employer basis or on a multiemployer or association basis. For many years Ford companies around the world had a firm policy against joining any business association for any purpose unless compelled by law to do so. One result was that Ford companies bargained with unions on a company basis even in countries where association bargaining was almost a universal practice.

Ford's general policy on employer associations was abandoned some years ago. Subsequently, the German and British companies studied the desirability of joining in on the association bargaining that prevailed in the auto industries of their respective countries. The German company decided to participate. This decision was based on such factors as the applicable laws, the bargaining structure employed, how the association operated, the results and stability achieved, and the likely problems of an individual company bargaining in light of what was known of union objectives. The British company, after considering similar factors and its own bargaining history, concluded that joining the association offered small hope for a net improvement and carried a substantial risk of making things worse. It therefore decided against joining the association bargaining arrangement even though the company's current practices were not ideal. In my judgment, both companies made correct decisions. To have maintained a flat ideological policy for or against such bargaining would have been a serious error. Indeed, in Belgium, one major Ford facility bargains on an association basis, while the other bargains on an individual basis. I see little reason to impose a global choice in such matters.

A second important conclusion has been that transnational transference of ideas is beset with dangers arising from sometimes subtle distinctions in terms and their differing connotations from country to country. For example, in regard to what subjects should be included in the collective bargaining relationship, there is extensive literature on the various issues about which management should "consult" with unions. I have the strong impression that even among countries where the word "consult" is a standard term in union-management parlance, its connotations are not uniform. "Consult" is not a standard term in the lexicon of U.S. union-management relations. Instead, we talk about what subjects should be "bargained" over.

This emphasis stems from the provisions of U.S. law requiring the parties to "bargain" with respect to "wages, hours, and other terms and conditions of employment," and ties a union's right to strike over an issue to its bargainability. The concept of bargainability is more rigid, and fraught with a good deal more danger to management, than the basic concept of consultation. This distinction accounts for the intensity and frequency of litigation over the required subject matter of bargaining unique to the United States. It must be kept clearly in mind when considering the application of other countries' practices to the United States and vice versa. Moreover, even in countries that share the "consultation"

concept, it is important to compare closely the exact implications that have attached to it in practice.

Additional examples could be cited, but those discussed
illustrate why detailed multinational prescriptions and rules
for employee relations and collective bargaining have not been
adopted for the various Ford operations around the world.
Another related judgment is that Ford should not, and
probably could not successfully, try to run employee relations
and collective bargaining in all the countries in which it
controls affiliates from Dearborn, Michigan. Those in
Dearborn probably would find it impossible to develop the
necessary knowledge, sensitivity, and relationships to do it
well, even if they wanted to take on the task.

But there is a more important factor that supports the
continuing responsibility and authority of the affiliated
companies to handle these matters. Without this responsibility, it would be extremely difficult, if not impossible, for the
affiliates to develop and maintain the kinds of relationships
with their employees and employee representatives that are a
key factor in the success of their operations. The requisites for
building effective local relationships are neglected in the
current debate on macrobargaining structures. While some
transnational union organizations are attempting to bring
about fundamental changes in the present arrangements, I
continue to believe that they are sound and should be preserved.

It does not follow, however, that one should ignore what is
going on in the affiliated companies and leave them in
isolation. On the contrary, Ford makes every effort to assure
that they are as well prepared and well equipped as possible to
carry out their responsibilities. Even though there are many
differences among countries, there are far more similarities
with respect both to labor relations and to the operational
requirements of the business. For example, preserving management flexibility to meet the challenge of competitive and
changing market conditions is of fundamental importance
wherever such conditions exist—and if there are any markets

now where such conditions do not exist, they are likely to develop in the future. Yielding to wildcat strike pressures for concessions is asking for more trouble anywhere. Shortsighted work practices or concessions to unions that can be "lived with" at the moment become burdensome when conditions change, and are most difficult to remedy in every national context. Accordingly, Ford seeks to ensure that all Ford officials involved understand the fundamentals and carefully analyze proposed actions for consistency with them.

The emphasis on fundamentals has been particularly important for affiliates in countries in which motor vehicle markets have been in transition to the kind of mass markets we have long had in the United States. It is vital that local management understands the implications of such developments for the operating needs of their companies and hence for what they do or do not do in collective bargaining. Ford also tries to make sure local managers have the benefit of knowledge and experience gained by any of the Ford companies in dealing with particular demands, provisions, or practices, and that they are informed about the relevant developments among unions on the international front. Interchange of information and experience for mutual consideration has become extremely important to all company participants in bargaining process.

Finally, but by no means least important, Ford seeks to make sure that its affiliates have bright, competent people dealing with matters in this area of responsibility who take the well-researched, analytical, objective approach that is a prerequisite to sound actions.

Pressures from the union side, as noted, are another aspect of our subject. There is nothing new, of course, in the existence of transnational bodies and mechanisms in the trade union movement. The notion of international solidarity among workers has a long historical tradition, and has long been institutionalized in support of ideology, political influence, and the organization of larger numbers of workers. In recent years, as we all know, there has been a growing trend toward adding the specific objectives, terms, strategies, tactics, and targets of collective bargaining to these transnational union bodies, and toward adapting old mechanisms or fashioning new ones for bargaining purposes. It is important to remember that these activities are supplemental to, not a substitution for, the other functions of such labor groups.

This trend was not unexpected in view of the growing competition of world markets, the increasing internationalization of business, and the general "shrinking" of the world. Not surprisingly, Ford was selected as one of the international labor movement's guinea pigs, providing a unique opportunity to watch the unions at close range. Although union groups generally offer the growth of multinational corporations as the explanation for their actions, close examination indicates that this factor is at least as much a rationalization as a justification.

The original impetus for the testing of Ford policies came primarily from American unions—particularly the auto and electrical workers—and in my view this reflected, more than anything else, a concern about growing competition in U.S. markets from foreign producers with far lower hourly labor rates. This concern grew regardless of whether or not foreign competitors were affiliated with American companies; unaffiliated competitors were also acquiring technology and economies of scale. I note this point not for defensive reasons, but to demonstrate that the efforts of unions, and whatever effects may flow from these efforts on collective bargaining in various countries, will not be confined to affiliates of multinational companies—even though the latter might be targeted for special treatment in certain respects.

As indicated, Ford has had some experience as one of those targets. Some years ago the United Auto Workers instigated the formation of a "world" automotive council under the umbrella of the International Metal Trades Federation. The council comprises several subcouncils, one of which consists of delegates from unions representing Ford employees in many countries. It has been effective in facilitating information exchange and other forms of communication. The UAW has made efforts through this and other mechanisms to intervene at corporate headquarters on behalf of unions having disputes in other countries. Although statements have circulated that these efforts have met with some success, facts prove the contrary. Ford sees no merit in establishing the UAW and the parent company as the final step in a world-wide grievance procedure. Such an arrangement would be not only inadvisable but also harmful to sound labor relations at home and abroad.

These developing transnational union mechanisms are bound to grow in importance and significance. There are, however, some aspects of the picture which prevent one from envisioning rapid movement to joint negotiations or bargaining uniformity on the union side. For one thing, we can expect unions in countries with advantageous competitive situations to be wary of advice from those less advantaged. Moreover, unions that vote for fine-sounding resolutions at international gatherings often do not find it practical to adhere closely to these pronouncements when they get home. This is particularly true in developed countries where union policies and philosophy, as well as bargaining institutions and practices, are encrusted with tradition and exist in differing frameworks of law and expectations.

On the other hand, analytical foresight is clouded by uncertainty as to how much weight should be accorded to tradition and traditional expectations in judging how the contending forces will balance out. The future shape of collective bargaining in various countries will probably be influenced by forces other than the formation of new transnational mechanisms for close liaison by union leaders. The net effect of national traditions, political and economic forces, and such structural innovations as the Common Market is yet to be seen. The minimum to be expected from the new international labor organizations is the exchange of information and ideas about contract provisions, workplace practices, bargaining practices and objectives, dispute settlement procedures, negotiating strategies, tactics, and techniques. This will be especially true of those business sectors producing goods or services that compete in world markets. Sophistication and feelings of togetherness will be enhanced.

We can expect greater pressures than ever before for the selective adoption or elaboration in one country of precedents set in another. How far and how fast matters will proceed beyond this minimum, if at all, must be rated rather speculative at this point. My own view is that transnational union bodies will not for some time seek substitute bargaining mechanisms to replace the national systems now in use. Instead they will seek a supplementary role, intruding into areas not presently bargained.

For example, the most recent approach to Ford by the International Metalworkers Federation was a proposal to set up a mechanism for discussing plans for future investment and production at either the European or parent-company level. Before rejecting it, Ford gave the union secretariat an opportunity to demonstrate why this would be advantageous to Ford. The presentation reinforced some of the tentative conclusions I had already reached. First, the proposals were designed to be an entering wedge, and thus were initially put forward in innocuous terms. Second, there was a heavy component of ideological views in them. And third, the basic thrust was to bring about effective and forceful union participation in making decisions that Ford believed its interests, and those of the public, required that it not share with unions. I think it is clear that unions are poorly suited to deal with business decisions of this kind. This is not because they are manned by rascals—though this can happen too—but because of their inherent characteristics and preoccupations as unions.

Finally, a brief comment on drawing general inferences about multinational corporations from the characteristics and experiences of any one of them. Corporations have affiliated operations in more than one country for all sorts of reasons and in many different ways. The term *multinational* has come into use to denote but one characteristic that a large number of otherwise quite disparate and independently guided businesses happen to share. They are, as a group, an unorganized, disorganized, and motley lot which would be well-advised to exercise a bit of caution in their dealings with international labor.

Part 5
The Emerging System

9

Putting National Employment Policy on the Bargaining Table

Ernest G. Green

It has been clearly demonstrated that labor, business, community groups, and local leaders can work together for urban revitalization. The collective bargaining process is crucially important to the achievement of certain social goals today, perhaps chief among them the reduction and redistribution of urban unemployment through various manpower training programs.

Collective bargaining, in the first instance, is a form of democratic self-government that has both intrinsic philosophical value and practical utility. Not only does it make it possible for workers to organize and bargain collectively through representatives of their own choosing, but it also helps management solve management problems. The Carter administration is attempting to strengthen collective bargaining legislation, and the chances of its doing so look pretty good. By creating stiffer penalties for violators of the National Labor Relations Act and by speeding up the union election process, it should be easier for workers to realize their rights and it should become more costly for companies to disobey the law.

Collective bargaining, in the second instance, is a promising means for addressing larger issues than "wages, hours, and working conditions" in the traditional sense. The administration is therefore attempting to make it easier for collective bargaining to deal with problems beyond the scope of the parties involved—problems such as inflation, unemployment, overall productivity, international trade, and occupational safety. We need to develop effective mechanisms to do this, like cooperative committees in particular industries. In Chicago, for instance, the Department of Labor found that seasonality in the construction industry was often due to force of habit rather than to bad weather, and as a result we were able to pace contracting activity more evenly. Such mechanisms can supplement collective bargaining, narrow the range of conflict, and facilitate focusing on other problems.

With respect to the nation's unemployment problem, there has never been a time in American history when the kind of cooperative effort that collective bargaining represents has been more necessary than it is right now. With the national jobless rate near 7 percent, with Black unemployment at 13.1 percent, with unemployment for all teenagers at 18.1 percent, and with unemployment for Black teenagers at an abysmal 37.4 percent, it is obvious that our work is cut out for those of us in the public and private sectors who bear responsibility for employment policy.

Without full employment, which Secretary of Labor Ray Marshall aptly defines as the situation where no American worker has to look very long for a productive job, we will continue to experience human misery and economic deprivation. It is estimated that for every percentage point of unemployment, the federal treasury loses $16 billion in tax revenue. Whenever American workers cannot work, the whole society suffers because it loses their output and because they have to be supported by other resources. We all know that the labor market is in a grave crisis. In a nation where there is still much job discrimination, where minority workers are disproportionately concentrated in areas of urban and rural poverty, where minority workers often lack education and training and are overrepresented in low-paying, less-skilled jobs, something is desperately wrong.

There are numerous issues associated with the unemployment crisis, but at bottom it involves something more compelling than faulty economic indicators, or even reduced production and lost tax revenue: behind every grim statistic in the monthly unemployment report lies a trail of thwarted hopes and broken spirits. It was for all these reasons that President Carter made an economic stimulus package his first and most important order of business. And when he was finally able to sign the Economic Stimulus Appropriations Act in May 1977, it meant that the Department of Labor's Employment and Training Administration could move quickly from planning to actual implementation on two major employment initiatives: 1) a massive expansion of public service employment, and 2) substantial increases and improvements in job training. I would like to outline where we stand on these initiatives and how employment policy relies heavily on private sector involvement, especially in the collective bargaining process.

Our job-training initiative for youth specifically provides for key roles to be played by schools, businesses, and unions. One example is our twentyfold expansion of the summer Vocational Exploration Program, in which we worked with the National Alliance of Businessmen and the Human Resources Development Institute to enhance job opportunities for 5,000 young people in 1978. Another example is our effort to develop a variety of subsidies to private not-for-profit employers for youth employment and to develop new apprenticeship agreements with unions. Also, the new youth programs include set-asides for in-school projects and for the development of better labor market information for young people—a fact of no small significance when we consider that more than 700,000 teenagers drop out of high school every year. Another initiative to assist young people is our expansion of the Job Corps from 60 centers to 130 centers. This will serve about 65,000 young people, nearly 75 percent of them minority group members.

As is well known, industries and unions are actively involved in the operation of Job Corps centers. We propose, for example, to increase labor and business linkages with Job Corps graduates and trainees by exploring opportunities for paid work for enrollees. There will be about five new centers in New York alone, serving between 2,500 and 3,200 young people.

One of the key components of our veterans' initiatives is the HIRE (Help through Industry Retraining and Employment) program. Under this program, many major corporations will be employing and training large numbers of veterans. The first HIRE agreement was with the Chicago and Northwestern Railroad, which is going to employ 432 Vietnam-era veterans in twenty occupations. Several more major agreements have since been signed, and I know that many companies in the New York metropolitan area will want to participate in this priority program.

In our apprenticeship initiatives, we are working with numerous businesses and unions to expand and extend apprenticeship in industries where it is weak or nonexistent, and to create more apprenticeship opportunities for women and minorities. Among these initiatives are the funding of continuation training for unemployed apprentices and journeymen; greater linkages between secondary schools and apprenticeship; partial offsets of training costs in industries where apprenticeship does not exist or where it is underutilized; legislative proposals to strengthen the National Apprenticeship Act; and amendment of equal employment rules in apprenticeship to require affirmative action for women.

To improve training in the construction industry in particular, we have proposed regulations to more effectively safeguard the welfare of participants in all of our training programs. These regulations, published in the Federal Register, cover standards, wage rates, safety, quality and minimum duration of training, equal opportunity, and affirmative action. They are designed to create many more job opportunities in construction, particularly in nonunion areas.

The new Skill Training Improvement Program is a tailored

employment program that enables operators of our programs to go to employers to determine the specific skills they need and then to train people for those skills. It is expected to benefit about 50,000 long-term jobless workers. It is designed with upgrading in mind and provides enough flexibility to bring this about.

A completely different initiative is represented by the tremendous expansion of public service employment (PSE) based on recognizing that the private sector is still the primary source of new jobs, but it is necessary to increase assistance to those for whom private sector jobs are unavailable. The PSE expansion is massive and direct. More than $6.5 billion has already been appropriated for it between now and the end of fiscal 1978. The expansion will take us from 310,000 PSE jobs to 725,000 by December of 1977, so that we can make a significant, speedy impact on economic recovery.

Public Service Employment does not represent a makeshift effort, and we must ensure that PSE jobs are not make-work. They must be meaningful jobs that provide participants with work experience readily transferable to the private sector. In many cases PSE jobs will also provide benefits to the PSE worker's community. Businesses, unions, schools, and governmental units at all levels can contribute significantly to the design and success of PSE projects. There is enough to be done in our society without usurping the work of regular government and private employers, but the overwhelming reaction to PSE openings makes it clear that the unemployed desperately want to work and that we must focus particularly on the problem of Black unemployment.

The special project undertaken in New York City following the 1977 blackout exemplifies the type of useful work that can be done under PSE expansion, and also exemplifies the overwhleming reaction just mentioned. With $2 million in Title VI funds, nearly 2,000 people were hired to clean up and restore affected areas. Many thousands more showed up looking for work. A substantial proportion of the expanded

PSE projects are concerned with weather-proofing, which conserves energy and helps those who cannot afford the work required, like elderly people living on fixed incomes. A notable example is in Union County, New Jersey, where five community-based organizations have joined together in a project to winterize about 150 houses of low-income families and the elderly. The project is to be funded by $300,000 in Title VI monies, with additional funding from Title I, the Older Americans Act, and local contributions. Participants will receive training to prepare them for unsubsidized jobs in modernization and home repair.

The PSE train to a more equitable and productive labor market is on the track and gaining speed. By early September 1977, there were more than half a million participants already on board—a figure very close to the total of all prime-sponsor hiring planned for that date. New York is right on schedule in its efforts to increase city-wide participation from 13,000 to 27,000 and state-wide participation from 27,000 to 64,000 by February 1978.

The Public Service Employment effort is as important as any employment and training program undertaken by this nation. As the foundation for the job component of the administration's welfare reform proposals, it is expected to provide 1.4 million slots annually by 1981, meaning about 2.5 million participants annually. The purpose of these proposals is to get jobs for those who can work and to give adequate income support to those who cannot and should not work.

The PSE programs tie in directly with our efforts to raise the minimum wage. As the minimum wage rises to $2.65 by 1978 and then in yearly steps to $3.35 at the beginning of 1981, we will go a long way toward establishing a labor market where people will make significantly more for working than for not working. In conjunction with welfare reform provisions for paying 15 percent of the participants 25 percent above the minimum wage for being work supervisors, and with 10 percent state supplements of the minimum wage, we feel that this will help us meet our 1981 goal for the job component of welfare reform. That goal is to ensure that every family with children and with one parent employed in the regular economy will have a minimum income 20 percent above the poverty line, and that every family with children and with one parent in subsidized employment will have a minimum income 13 percent above the poverty line.

Right now, people who make the minimum wage work for less than the poverty wage. It is important to remember that a great many of the workers who will benefit from our minimum wage proposals are not members of unions and have very limited power to improve their wages. The last change in the minimum wage was in 1974. If you ask yourself what position you would be in if you had not had a wage increase since then— particularly in view of inflation—the need for minimum wage increases becomes evident.

Another very important measure directly related to the participants in collective bargaining is intensification through the federal/state employment service system of the Job Service Improvement Program (JSIP). This will help us to continue our strong emphasis on services to employers and to keep getting their ideas on how we can improve. Excellent accomplishments have been made through such things as local employer committees and the account executive approach. Four new JSIP sites have recently been established in New York State—in Cortland, Syracuse, Poughkeepsie, and Middletown.

It is clear, then, that there are many ways in which the private sector can help stem the tide of runaway joblessness. It is very possible, for instance, that maximum private sector involvement would mean that our expansion of public service employment, and our acceleration of that expansion, would prove to be temporary measures. We would all be deluding ourselves, however, if we believed that private sector involvement is anywhere near what it could be. Capital investment has not risen as rapidly as expected, whether because of uncertainty about the economy, environmental concerns, or high energy costs. Profits have grown steadily and automobiles and housing have made strong gains, but goals with respect to Black and youth unemployment are far from being met.

It is my belief, and I know this belief is shared by Secretary Marshall and President Carter, that this nation can reduce unemployment, stimulate business, and minimize inflation at the same time. Our substantial public commitment is designed to accomplish these objectives. We also believe that since the entire American economic system is based on rewarding business for taking calculated risks, those who consider themselves entrepreneurs will want to invest more heavily in the nation's future. At the same time, those who represent organized labor will see that support for subsidized training, PSE programs, and the like will in the long run benefit all participants in the labor market.

The business executive and the union leader must recognize that increased and improved employment serves both their interests. We therefore pay close attention to productivity, efficient administration, and cost savings as the measures of viable employment policies. Job training and PSE employment can also produce significant returns for people and government while enabling economic growth to create lasting employment opportunities. The cooperation of labor and management in the employment programs I have described is imperative today since increasing numbers of Americans are entering the labor force and seeking gainful, meaningful jobs. While this trend reflects the impact of inflation on family incomes, it also reflects rising expectations created by solid labor market improvements in late 1976 and early 1977.

If we fail in further reducing the severity of unemployment and underemployment, we run the risk of American workers, particularly young workers, concluding that since they cannot work for the system, the system cannot work for them. Let us continue to fight in the institutions of government, in the offices of management, and in the private work place to ensure that does not happen.

10
Putting the Quality of Working Life on the Bargaining Table

Jerome M. Rosow

American attitudes toward work and lifestyles, perhaps the least examined of the determinants of labor relations, have undergone dramatic changes during the past decade. These changes are not transitory, but instead represent new values that will have a lasting effect upon the motivation and performance of people at work in our society and of the collective bargaining system in which their new interests are represented.

The new issues on the bargaining table are remarkably qualitative as compared to the largely quantitative concern with higher wages expressed in the past. Labor has traditionally entered into contract negotiations with an easily articulated position: "More." Management's practical and equally simple response has been "Less." Today perhaps the most important issues that arise flow from the demands of working people for an improved quality of life in the work place and from the demands of corporate managers for greater productivity.

For the present I would like to concentrate on the qualitative aspect of work rather than on production, since the latter has been more fully discussed generally and elsewhere in this volume. But some initial observations may apply equally to both questions. Since the quality of work is less easily measured than the wage rate or the hours of work, "better" is more difficult to define than "more." Humanistic cultural values, rather than economic ones, are increasingly the issue, but they are not widely understood.

The changing attitudes of labor and management have therefore created a new cultural dimension in the bargaining system that in turn synergistically affects these attitudes. I would like to examine the emerging attitudes of working Americans in terms of several aspects to which we may refer in shorthand form: the challenge of authority; the loss of confidence in institutions; the resistance to change; the changing attitudes toward work; the changed relationship between work and the family; and the slower pace of change in the work place than in society at large.

During the 1960s the United States and other Western societies experienced a so-called youth counterculture movement. Many of the traditionally radical attitudes of youth were intensified by a concern over environment and a revulsion against war. The revolution in social values has continued, so that the ideas originally advanced by a comparatively small number of students are now embraced by millions of young people in mainstream America.

As a by-product of these fundamental changes, American young people have changed their attitudes toward authority. In 1969 almost 70 percent of the young accepted authority with few reservations. Now, 70 percent say that they need not take orders from a supervisor at work if they disagree with the orders. Permissive Western society has fostered a change in authority roles. We have seen this change in schools and universities, where the young openly disagree with and challenge their teachers. In fact, during 1976 approximately 65,000 teachers were physically attacked in their classrooms. We have witnessed changes in the family, where traditional authority figures have adopted more open relationships with their children to achieve consent and stability. These values have carried over into marriage; the husband-wife relationship is undergoing a transformation.

It is to be expected that these changes in authority relationships would spread to the work place. But even though
younger, more educated workers resent authoritarianism, they
are not opposed to the proper exercise of authority. This
distinction is important. They respect authority when properly
exercised with restraint and rationality, but they reject
authority when it is abusive or arbitrary. This poses a challenge
for large bureaucratic organizations; they must rationalize
their work procedures and learn the art of managing with
consent.

In the United States the decline in respect for authority is
related to a growing mistrust of institutions. Business,
government, labor, the church, and the military have all fallen
in the general public's esteem. This mistrustful feeling is most
pronounced with regard to the presidency and big business,
two American institutions believed to possess the greatest
power in the country. Mistrust of corporations rose from 30
percent to 70 percent by 1975. In fact, by 1975 nine out of ten
U.S. citizens expressed a general mistrust of "those in power,"
covering business, government and, implicitly, most national
institutions. Some of this same cynicism is reflected in Western
European countries.

As recently as the mid-1960s, American big business enjoyed
a reputation for unmatched industrial know-how and technological achievement. This image of relative infallibility was
badly shaken by the financial failures of several multi-billion
dollar corporations. Business suffered post-Watergate shocks
when hundreds of companies were cited for illegal political
contributions. In addition, general mistrust toward big
business is no longer limited to the public at large, but also
applies to managerial employees. In one recent study, for
example, it was found that more than two-thirds of management within large organizations do not believe or support the
advertising programs of their own companies.

When a cherished institution falls from grace, when directors
are dismissed or charged with civil suits and found guilty,

when the ethics of the corporation are brought into question, what happens to the attitudes and loyalties of its own members? Employees are the first line of defense. Yet instead of acting in this capacity, many feel that they are the last to know of improprieties.

In contemporary demands for "corporate social responsibility," the private corporation increasingly recognizes that in addition to its basic economic role it must be responsive to the social needs of consumers, environmentalists, and of its own employees. Insofar as any of these have been badly neglected or subordinated to economic pressures and profit goals, they weaken public support for business as an institution and especially for companies that have violated the moral code.

This period of struggle to regain public support and sustain confidence offers institutions a new opportunity to restructure the work environment. Employees are basically gregarious social beings. People are drawn to work by both economic and social needs. Employees identify with the company, and they have a natural desire to belong to and be part of the work group, the department, and the larger organization. Their loyalties are reinforced by job security needs.

The U.S. Census estimates that 32 percent of American workers today are single (up from 27 percent in 1950): divorced, separated, widowed, or never married. Loneliness is a problem faced by a growing proportion of the labor force. The weakening of the American family reinforces this trend. The decline of the family, the church, and the small community has increased the importance of the work place for providing social support and a sense of involvement with other people in a common enterprise—for making life generally more meaningful.

Industrial workers dislike and fear change. Most of us, in our normal day-to-day activities, are sensitive to change; we are uncomfortable with a disruption of our established routines. For example, people find it difficult to change a commuting pattern. Within the work place, change introduces the unknown. Since the individual worker has a limited degree of control over his work and his future, it is difficult to accept change without a feeling of insecurity. Usually workers feel that change imposed from above is intended to meet the goals of management, to increase production, or to reduce costs, rather than to improve working conditions, reduce stress or increase opportunity, pay, and security.

Many students of Japanese labor relations believe that the strong employment security provided by the individual employer has contributed to high growth in plant productivity. Since employees in Japan feel secure and essentially have lifetime employment, they do not resist change.

By contrast, in other industrial nations new technology and production processes often displace some of the work force. Also, external economic forces of competition and cyclical declines threaten layoffs. In the short run, then, the penalties of change may outweigh the rewards—this applies to workers and managers alike. Society has been searching for better ways of managing the human costs of change so that the full burden does not fall on the worker. Where the full employment philosophy is deeply embedded, as in Japan and Sweden, change is less threatening.

Although we tend to think of workers as the principal obstacle to change, the fact is that supervisors and middle managers are often more of an obstacle. This is easy to understand since they are often caught in the middle. Supervisors rarely participate in the decisions to change. Yet they are expected to carry out the change. Further, they themselves are threatened by the new and unknown and often feel as insecure as the average worker.

The work ethic had its origins in the beginning of western civilization. The early Greeks regarded work as a curse. It suggested drudgery, heavy heartedness, and exhaustion. For the Hebrews it was regarded as an atonement for original sin. The early Christians followed this concept—work was considered an act of expiation. They also looked to it as a means

of spreading charity or sharing worldly goods with the
needy.

Protestantism injected moral meaning into the work ethic
when Luther conceived of work as a way to serve God. Calvin
considered dislike of work sinful. The influence of the
"Protestant Work Ethic" continues in Switzerland to this day.
In a recent public referendum, the people preferred to remain
on a forty-five-hour work week instead of a forty-hour week.
The industrial revolution was fortified by the work ethic with
its explicit religious and moral connotations.

People today are not as prepared to tolerate adverse
conditions, hard, unrewarding work, and self-sacrifice for
rewards in an afterlife. This is not an antireligious view but
rather one supported by increased knowledge of the vastness of
the universe and growing skepticism about the immortality of
man. Thus the deferred gratification of pleasure is less
acceptable to many in the "now" generation. Hedonism, "the
gratification of pleasure-seeking instincts," according to
Webster's, is more in vogue.

In 1973, eight out of every ten American students believed
that "it's very important to do any job well." Daniel
Yankelovich's attitude surveys of youth have revealed con-
sistently that the work ethic is strong and alive, despite the
revolution in social values. However, youth's appraisal of the
traditional rewards of hard work has certainly changed. In
1967, a 69 percent majority answered "yes" to the question:
"Does hard work always pay off?" By 1975, 75 percent of
American students answered the question "no." This view of
the world of work may be realistic: many jobs are routine, dull,
and boring, and do not challenge the talents of the average
worker.

Yet this dramatic shift in attitudes is not easy to explain. Nor
does it suggest that the new breed of workers is less motivated. It
does reflect cynicism, higher expectations, and a questioning
attitude toward the value of work. It also places a more difficult
task upon managers to develop a commitment to the job and to
the organization. One leading student of this development

points out that many executives are seeking a new balance between work and the rest of life. Fewer executives take their attaché cases home every night, proof that their personal time is free from company work obligations.

It is believed that older workers, of my generation, are dedicated to the work ethic. If you are wondering whether the "new" cynicism is purely a function of age, in one survey workers over the age of fifty-five were asked whether they felt that they had a sense of achievement and reward looking back over their careers. The majority answered "No." Hard work did not pay off for them. They were also asked what they would like to change. "Nothing," they replied. They felt they were past that point in their working careers—it was too late—they would rather retire and leave the battleground to someone younger who might have sufficient years ahead to change the system.

Retirement data confirms this opinion. The labor force participation rate of men aged 55 to 64 has declined sharply— from 89 percent to 80 percent in 1977. This withdrawal of men in the prime of their working lives is a remarkable fact. One may also note that younger women are rushing in to seek the jobs older men no longer want.

Japan is considered by many the model industrial state in terms of productivity. The Japanese work ethic is often contrasted to that of the United States, a country believed to have declining work values. But according to a 1976 OED study, there are significant changes in attitudes among Japanese workers that reflect a falling off in traditional devotion to work and the enterprise, especially among the young. From 1930 to 1968 the number of Japanese who concurred with the statement, "Don't think about money or fame; just live a life that suits your own tastes," increased from 11 percent to 51 percent. During the same period, those agreeing that it was wise to "Resist all evils in the world and live a pure and just life," dropped from 30 percent to 10 percent.

A survey of workers' attitudes toward life indicated that 40 percent valued work more highly than family life or leisure, but for males under twenty and females under thirty, leisure was most highly valued. In 1974, 60 percent of workers surveyed were not satisfied with their wages. Additionally, 40 percent wanted to change jobs. These findings show that the changing attitudes of the young are not peculiar to the United States, and that work must compete with other values.

Western industrialized societies have been riding the crest of economic growth. Although this crest peaked in 1974, it has not diminished deep-seated and almost universal expectations of a rising standard of living.

Enjoying a burst of consumer goods production and a progressive rise in purchasing power, Europeans and Americans alike have cultivated the desire for more and more goods, and for a better life. Consumer attitudes have been sharpened by the production and distribution of massive quantities of attractive goods. These include quick-frozen convenience foods; labor-saving machines in the home; the private automobile, including the second and third family car; year-round and summer homes; and increased leisure and glamorous vacations. The significant advance in the real standard of living has been almost uninterrupted since World War II. The new generation of workers and their children have been conditioned by this boom economy to perceive these advantages as normal.

Expectations have become entitlements. Western governments have expanded social services in health, welfare, housing, and education, and have provided broad income transfer programs to shelter individuals and families against economic hardship, unemployment, illness, or aging. People in Western societies have learned to believe that they are "entitled" to the direct allocation of resources through their political systems as a supplement to the economic system. The world-wide recession of 1974-75, still persisting in many countries, did not alter these expectations. In fact, many political programs expanded as the economic system fell into recession. The economic slowdown, rising unemployment, and problems of inflation are seen as temporary phenomena that introduce, at worst, a pause in the fulfillment of the era of rising entitlements. In 1975, 56 percent of the American public expressed the view that, as a matter of right, they are entitled to an ever-increasing standard of living.

Today's workers are members of the affluent society. Better educated, with even higher expectations for their careers, they want more, faster. They are impatient for advancement in money and status; they want more openness, more communication, and more involvement. And they expect this as an entitlement, not as something to be earned over many years of loyal service.

Changing attitudes toward work, combined with the revolution in social values, have raised new interest in improving the quality of work life. The expectations and aspirations of workers require a social agenda with heavy economic undertones. It involves a shift away from the authoritarian concept of management toward one that places a higher value on individual employees and groups as critical factors in work efficiency. This new agenda stands in sharp contrast to the dominant contemporary practices of work organization. Many terms have been used to describe the newer concepts, including worker participation, participatory management, industrial democracy, autonomous work groups and work teams, humanization of work, job redesign and job enrichment, and the quality of working life.

It is increasingly thought that the more useful and lasting changes will be those that embrace the entire environment of work and seek to achieve a systematic restructuring of the organization of work relationships. As a comprehensive concept, the quality of working life encompasses such matters as the organization of work, that is, of the production process itself, hierarchical structures, relations with workmates, the social situation within the firm, the working environment, participation in decision-making at all levels, and opportunities for self-development and advancement.

Employment policies and operating practices can be accommodated to the rising expectations of employees. Employees desire opportunity, participation, and the use of their potential. These are universal human needs. Workers want to learn, to receive training, and to develop on the job. They want more meaningful participation in decisions that affect their work. Such participation can be linked to productive goals; it need not become an undermining of authority or a dilution of management control. Under proper conditions, employee participation increases motivation and builds a commitment to the goals of the enterprise. Social interaction is also important.

The growing involvement of minorities, adolescents, and women in the work place, of multiple worker families and single parent families, and other aspects of demographic changes in the work force have numerous implications for the cultural dimension of collective bargaining. First, they clearly point to the growing popularity and need for flexible working hours, including staggered hours, flextime, and shorter work weeks. Many of these changes can be accomodated by employers with no capital investment, with a minimum effect on present production programs, and with payouts in reduced absenteeism, lower turnover, and higher productivity. These changes also point to a need for part-time jobs for women, younger workers, and older workers. We will witness increasing husband/wife career conflicts and maladjustments. Many companies have revised their policies to permit the employment of both husbands and wives without regard to previous restrictions on nepotism, a hangover from the depression; and transfers and management development programs must increase in flexibility to recognize the combined needs of both spouses as their careers are important to the firm as well as to the family.

There has been some experimentation with shared jobs, where husbands and wives with the same profession share one job. Sweden has acknowledged the impact of husband/wife working by providing seven month's maternity leave that can be shared by both parents. This experiment is worth watching, since it reflects the concern of society with this problem.

Changes in Western society have been more rapid and penetrating than have been changes within the work place. Changes in mores, folkways, and laws have reflected the revolution in social values. By contrast, conditions have remained relatively static in the work place. The large bureaucracies of government, industry, churches, universities, and the military all remain relatively resistant to change. Authoritarian rules and customs are deeply embedded and are shielded from the outside environment. Sheltered from the winds and torrents of social change, the organization business-men continue to respond best to the internal sounds of the cloistered world where they work. Corporate leadership is angry and confused by many external social changes and views them as an unwelcome disruption of the relative tranquility of the past and a threat to efficiency.

Nevertheless, the concern for human values must be focused on the work place, first because individuals devote the greater part of their mature lifetimes to their occupations; their time and energy are deeply engaged in this endeavor. Second, our freedom, growth, and standard of living depend upon earned income. Third, the role of breadwinner is fundamental to the family and to self respect in society. Fourth, human resources are the only natural resources not in scarce supply. Finally, and most important of all, production, industrial growth, and technological advances are not ends in themselves. They are a means to an end, namely, improving the quality of life for all.

Appendixes

APPENDIX A:
The Personal Dimension—
Biographies of the Contributors

Wayne L. Horvitz
Federal Mediation and Conciliation Service

Wayne Horvitz became the ninth director of the Federal Mediation and Conciliation Service (FMCS) in 1977.

Horvitz was chairman of the Joint Labor-Management Committee of the Retail Food Industry from its inception in 1974 until he became FMCS director. He also served as a member of the National Commission on Productivity and the Quality of Work Life.

From 1969 to 1974 he was an independent arbitrator, mediator, and consultant on labor-management, legislative, and public affairs in Washington, D.C. He served as a public member, vice chairman, and chairman of the Food Industry Tripartite Wage and Salary Committee of the Cost of Living Council from 1973 to 1974.

Horvitz was director and then vice president of industrial relations for the Matson Navigation Company in San Francisco from 1960 to 1967, and was the company's vice president for government liaison from 1967 to 1969.

He was employed by the General Cable Corporation of new York City in 1947, and was their associate director of personnel and labor relations from 1953 to 1957. From 1957 to 1960 he was an assistant professor at Arizona State University, a founding partner of Western Management Consultants, and an arbitrator. He has been a member of the Industrial Relations Research Association and the American Management Association.

Born on October 8, 1920, in Chicago, he received his bachelor's degree from Bard College, Columbia University, in 1942. He was an Alfred P. Sloan Fellow at the Massachusetts Institute of Technology, receiving a master of science degree in 1953. He served as an enlisted man in the U.S. Army in North Africa and Europe during World War II.

Horvitz is married, the father of four children, and resides in Washington, D.C.

William W. Winpisinger
International Association of Machinists

In 1977 William Winpisinger was elected president of the million-member International Association of Machinists and Aerospace Workers (IAM), one of the oldest and largest unions in North America.

Winpisinger was born in 1924 in Cleveland, Ohio, where his father was a journeyman printer. He dropped out of high school during World War II to join the Navy, where he learned his trade as an automotive diesel mechanic. After the war he returned to Cleveland, went to work as an auto mechanic, and joined IAM Automotive Lodge 1363.

Wimp, as he is known to thousands of machinists, became a shop steward, then a local lodge president, and in 1951 at the age of twenty-six, became one of the youngest members ever appointed to the IAM national field staff. Winpisinger was originally assigned to organizing auto mechanics in and around Cleveland. He later served as a negotiator, arbitrator, and troubleshooter in the Great Lakes area and then from IAM headquarters in Washington, D.C., where he assumed national responsibilities.

In 1965 he became the IAM national coordinator, with responsibility for some 120,000 members working in the auto and truck repair industry; in 1967 he was elected general vice president, with jurisdiction over the union's railroad and airline membership; and, prior to becoming international president, he served as resident vice president, or chief of staff, at IAM international headquarters.

Since assuming IAM leadership he has substantially expanded the union's civil rights, community services, job safety, public relations, and organizing programs. He has frequently testified before congressional committees on legislation affecting working people, and he considers himself somewhat to the left of most labor leaders. Winpisinger is president of the Institute of Collective Bargaining and Group Relations, Inc., advisor to the Federal Committee on Apprenticeship, trustee of the National Planning Association, member of the Finance Committee of the Democratic National Committee, and vice chairman of the American League for International Security Assistance.

Winpisinger is married and the father of five children. He resides in Silver Spring, Maryland.

Theodore W. Kheel
Institute of Collective Bargaining

Theodore Kheel has been an attorney specializing in the practice of labor law since 1937, and since 1949 he has been a partner in the New York City law firm of Battle, Fowler, Jaffin, Pierce & Kheel. He was a founder of and is currently administrative director for the Institute of Collective Bargaining and Group Relations, Inc.

Kheel graduated from college and law school at Cornell University. He has served widely as a mediator, arbitrator, and negotiator in labor relations. He was appointed by President Johnson to several presidential boards on national labor disputes from 1962 to 1966. He was a special consultant to the President's Commission on Equal Employment Opportunity (1962-63), a member of the President's Maritime Advisory Committee (1964-66), and a member of the President's National Citizens Committee for Community Relations (1964-68).

Among the many New York City and State positions Kheel has held in the area of employment are chairman of the Mayor's Committee on Job Advancement (1962-65) and special advisor to the mayor for labor relations (1974-77). He has acted as a mediator, fact-finder, and arbitrator in many public labor disputes, most notably New York City's 1966 Transport Workers Union strike.

Kheel was president of the National Urban League (1956-60) and is now president of the Center for Non-Broadcast Television, Inc. He is a director of Athlone Industries, Inc., UV Industries, Inc., and the Western Union Telegraph Company. He is the author of *Kheel on Labor Law* (1976), *Guide to Fair Employment Practices* (1964), *How Race Relations Affect Your Business* (1963), *Pros and Cons of Compulsory Arbitration* (1961), and *Transit and Arbitration* (1960).

A resident of New York City, where he was born in 1914, Kheel is married and the father of six children.

Glenn E. Watts
Communications Workers of America

Glenn Watts is president of the Communications Workers of America (CWA) and a member of the Executive Council of the AFL-CIO.

Born in Stony Point, North Carolina, in 1920, Watts started work as a telephone installer for the C&P Telephone Company and later became a service engineer. He took an active part in union activities and was elected a local president in 1948.

In 1951 he was elected director of CWA District 2 (Virginia, West Virginia, Pennsylvania, Delaware, Maryland, and the

District of Columbia). He became assistant to the president in 1956, executive vice president in 1965, and president of the 600,000-member CWA, the largest communications union in the world, in 1974.

Watts's primary concern throughout his career as a union officer has been collective bargaining. He was instrumental in formulating the CWA bargaining strategy that led eventually to national bargaining with AT&T in 1974. His international labor activities have included membership on the Executive Committee of the Postal Telegraph and Telephone International, the world-wide labor secretariat of telecommunications workers, and service as secretary-treasurer of the American Institute for Free Labor Development.

Watts, through his interest in social and economic progress, has served as vice chairman of the Board of Governors and chairman of the Executive Committee of the United Way of America; as a member of the President's Commission on Mental Health, as a member of the Trilateral Commission, treasurer of the National Urban Coalition, as a trustee of the Ford Foundation, and as a director of the Alliance to Save Energy.

Watts has been a resident of Washington, D.C., since the 1930s. He is married and has three children.

Benjamin F. Bailar
Former Postmaster General of the United States

Benjamin Bailar was Postmaster General of the United States from 1975 to 1978. He is now a director and executive vice president of United States Gypsum Company.

Born in Champaign, Illinois, in 1934, Bailar received a B.A. degree from the University of Colorado and an M.B.A. from Harvard Business School. After service as a Navy officer (1955-57), he was associated with Continental Oil Company (1959-62). He then worked with American Can Company (1962-72), rising to company vice president and then serving as president of the company's international subsidiary. Bailar's current responsibilities at United States Gypsum, the Chicago-based producer of building materials and industrial projects, include acting as chief financial officer.

Joining the Postal Service in 1972 as senior assistant postmaster general and chief financial officer, he became deputy postmaster general and a member of the Board of Governors in 1974. President Nixon appointed Bailar the sixty-first Postmaster General in 1975.

Bailar joined the Postal Service in the wake of the 1970 one-week postal strike, involving some 200,000 postal employees, after the passage of the Postal Reorganization Act, and during the term of the Service's first collective bargaining agreement (1971-73). He participated in the negotiations of the 1973 and 1975 agreements, which proceeded without work stoppages or third-party involvement of any kind. His efforts to reorganize the postal system included the development of a collective bargaining system to replace legislative regulation of postal employment.

Bailar is a director of Monmouth College (Illinois) and of the National Council on Alcoholism, Inc. He is an officer of the Boy Scouts of America. Bailar is married and the father of two children.

Albert Shanker
American Federation of Teachers

Albert Shanker is president of the American Federation of Teachers (AFT) and its New York City local, the United Federation of Teachers (UFT). He is a vice president and member of the AFL-CIO Executive Council.

Shanker was born in 1928 in New York City, where he attended the public schools. He graduated with honors from the University of Illinois and completed Ph.D. course requirements at Columbia University.

Shanker taught mathematics and philosophy in New York City schools from 1952 to 1964. He took an active role in the organization of New York City teachers by the UFT, and was very involved with the 1960 and 1961 strikes. Shanker helped win the first contract with the Board of Education in 1962. He was elected UFT president in 1964, and in 1968 led three lengthy city-wide strikes involving school decentralization.

With 70,000 members, the UFT is the largest local union in the world. The UFT and its state affiliate, the 200,000 member New York State United Teachers, are widely recognized as major forces in New York City and State politics. Shanker has played a prominent role in national affairs as president of the AFT and also has been an executive committee member of the Workers Defamation League and a director of the A. Philip Randolph Institute.

Shanker is married and the father of three children. He resides in Mamaroneck, New York.

Sol C. Chaikin
International Ladies' Garment Workers' Union

Sol Chaikin is president of the International Ladies' Garment Workers' Union (ILGWU) and a member of the Executive Council of the AFL-CIO.

Born in 1918, he was educated in the New York City public schools, attended the College of the City of New York, and graduated from Brooklyn Law School in 1940, at which time he became an organizer for the ILGWU.

Chick Chaikin, as he is widely known, held virtually every major administrative position in the Garment Workers' Union, from business agent for dressmaking shops to international vice president. In 1973 he was elected general secretary-treasurer, and two years later became president of the historical 350,000 member union.

Chaikin has been associated with a number of organizations,

including the New York and National Urban Coalition, the Coalition for New York, and the Brookings Institute. In international affairs, he has been a member of the Atlantic Council, the Trilateral Commission, and the United Nations Association of the U.S.A. He is past national chairman of the American Trade Union Council for Histadrut and was appointed by President Carter as a member of the U.S. delegation to the 1977 Belgrade Conference of the Commission for Security and Cooperation in Europe.

A resident of New York City, Chaikin is married and the father of three children.

Malcolm L. Denise
Former Vice President for Labor Relations,
Ford Motor Company

Malcolm Denise retired in 1975 as vice president for labor relations of Ford Motor Company. He is now counsel to the Detroit law firm of Keller, Thoma, Toppin & Schwarze.

Denise was born in Decatur, Michigan, in 1913. He received a B.A. and a J.D. from the University of Michigan. After joining Ford in 1941, Denise held a number of legal and executive positions and became vice president for labor relations in 1954. While at Ford he was an employer member of the National Wage Stabilization Board and of the United States delegation to the International Labor Organization. Denise has served as vice president of the American Management Association, as chairman of the Motor Vehicle Manufacturers Association Personnel Committee, and as a director of the Industrial Relations Research Association. He has been an active member of the Business Roundtable and the Chamber of Commerce.

One of Denise's principal concerns at Ford was the development and management of labor relations at Ford affiliates in some thirty countries around the world, including participation in multiemployer national bargaining. He is now cochairman of the International Labor Law Committee of the American Bar Association.

Denise has been a frequent participant in conferences and seminars, and has had papers published by the American Academy of Political and Social Science, the Bureau of National Affairs, the Commerce Clearing House, the University of Chicago, The Conference Board, New York University, and the Organization for Economic Cooperation and Development.

Denise is married and the father of six children. He resides in Grosse Pointe, Michigan.

<h2 style="text-align:center">Ernest G. Green
Assistant U.S. Secretary of Labor</h2>

Ernest Green was appointed Secretary of Labor for Employment and Training by President Carter in 1977.

Green was born in 1941 in Little Rock, Arkansas. He was one of the "Little Rock Nine" who integrated the public schools of that city under the protection of federal troops. He was the first Black to graduate from Central High School and went on to receive B.A. and M.A. degrees from Michigan State University. From 1962 to 1964, Green was a member of the Michigan State research team in Prince Edward County, Virginia, studying the effects on Black students of closing all the county public schools.

In 1964 he joined the Recruitment and Training Program (RTP, Inc.), formerly the Joint Apprenticeship Program of the Workers Defense League and A. Philip Randolph Educational Fund. Beginning as a field representative, attempting to place Black and Puerto Rican young men in construction apprenticeships, Green became executive director of RTP in 1967, greatly expanding the organization's university training programs.

As the chief officer of the Department of Labor for

employment and training, Green is responsible for a broad range of programs, including comprehensive training, public service employment, unemployment insurance, apprenticeship promotion, work incentive, alien worker certification, technical assistance, research, and development.

Among numerous honors, Green has received both the A. Philip Randolph and John D. Rockefeller awards. Green has two children and lives in Washington, D.C.

Jerome M. Rosow
Work in America Institute

Jerome Rosow is the founding president and a director of the Work in America Institute.

Born in Chicago, Illinois in 1919, Rosow graduated from the University of Chicago in 1942. He held personnel and compensation positions in the Department of the Army and War Assets Administration from 1942 to 1951, at which time he became policy director of the Salary Stabilization Board. In 1953 Rosow joined the Creole Petroleum Corporation in Venezuela.

From 1955 to 1966 he held a series of executive positions with Standard Oil Company of New Jersey; from 1966 to 1969 he was manager of employee relations for Esso Europe in London, England; and from 1971 to 1975 he was manager of public affairs planning for Exxon Corporation.

President Nixon appointed Rosow Assistant Secretary of Labor for Policy, Evaluation and Research in 1969, a position he held for two years. He has also served as chairman of the President's Advisory Committee on Federal Pay (1972-77), as a member of the National Commission on Productivity and Work Quality (1974-75), and in numerous other positions as a government advisor.

He is currently president of the Industrial Relations

Research Association, vice president of the Board of Trustees of the National Committee on Employment of Youth, a member of the Conference Board, and a member of or consultant to numerous groups. He is the editor of *The Worker and the Job: Coping With Change* (1974), and *American Men in Government* (1949), and is a contributor to *Bargaining Without Boundaries* (1974) and numerous periodicals.

Rosow is married, the father of two children, and lives in Scarsdale, New York.

Franklin J. Havelick
Deputy Counsel to the Mayor, New York City

Franklin Havelick is Deputy Counsel to Edward I. Koch, Mayor of New York City.

Havelick was born in 1947 in New York City, where he attended the public schools. He received a B.A. from Columbia College in 1968, served as a journalist in the Army from 1968 to 1970, and received a J.D. from Columbia Law School in 1973.

From 1973 to 1978 he practiced law with the New York firm of Nattle, Fowler, Jaffin, Pierce & Kheel, and was associated with Theodore W. Kheel. During this time he was adjunct professor of political science at the New York Institute of Technology, a University Fellow in political science at Columbia University, and a Ford Foundation Fellow in collective bargaining. Havelick received an M.A. in 1977 and is a Ph.D. candidate in political science at Columbia, where he is adjunct assistant professor of public affairs. He is the author of "Young Man Warren; An Historical Analysis of the Chief Justice," which appeared in the *Civil Liberties Review*.

In 1978 he was appointed Assistant to the Mayor for legal and policy matters including personnel, civil service, labor relations, Collective Bargaining, and the Emergency Financial Control Board. He was an associate member of the National

Labor Relations Task Force (1976-78), and counsel to the Institute of Collective Bargaining (1975-78).

As an arbitrator, Havelick is a member of the labor, commercial, family disputes, and community disputes panels of the American Arbitration Association. He is on the labor panel of the New York State Mediation Board, and the consumer panel of the Better Business Bureau. He is also a member of the American Bar Association and the American Political Science Association.

Havelick is single and resides in New York City.

The Statistical Dimension— Collective Bargaining Data*

Part 1
The State of the System

   1. *Input: Labor, Management, and Government*

*The figures in this appendix are based on data from the Bureau of Labor Statistics.

Part 3
The Political Dimension

5. *Depoliticizing the Bargaining Process*
6. *Repoliticizing the Bargaining Process*

Part 4
The International Dimension

Part 5
The Emerging System

Figure 1. Membership of National Unions, 1930-74[1]

Millions of members

[1] Excludes Canadian membership but includes members in other areas outside the United States. Members of AFL-CIO directly affiliated local unions are also included. Members of single-firm and local unaffiliated unions are excluded. For the years 1948-52, midpoints of membership estimates, which were expressed as ranges, were used.

133

Figure 2. Union Membership as a Percent of Total Labor Force and of Employees in
Nonagricultural Establishments, 1930-74

Percent

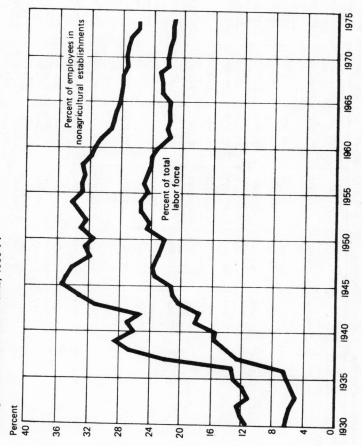

Figure 3. National unions and employee associations reporting 100,000 members or more, selected years, 1962-74[1]

Organization	1962	1964	1966	1968	1970	1972	1974
UNIONS							
Automobile (Ind.)	1,074,000	1,168,000	1,403,000	1,473,000	1,486,000	1,394,000	1,545,000
Bakery[2]	—	—	—	—	152,000	146,000	134,000
Boilermakers	125,000	125,000	140,000	140,000	138,000	132,000	138,000
Bricklayers	151,000	135,000	149,000	160,000	143,000	149,000	148,000
Carpenters	739,000	760,000	800,000	793,000	820,000	820,000	820,000
Chemical	82,000	85,000	93,000	104,000	101,000	85,000	85,000
Clothing[3]	376,000	377,000	382,000	386,000	386,000	365,000	350,000
Communications	279,000	294,000	321,000	357,000	422,000	443,000	499,000
District 50 (Ind.)[4]	—	210,000	232,000	232,000	210,000	—	—
Electrical (IBEW)	793,000	806,000	875,000	897,000	922,000	957,000	991,000
Electrical (IUE)	295,000	271,000	320,000	324,000	300,000	290,000	298,000
Electrical (UE) (Ind.)	163,000	165,000	167,000	167,000	163,000	165,000	163,000
Federal Employees (NFFE) (Ind.)	50,000	—	80,000	95,000	100,000	85,000	100,000
Fire Fighters	109,000	115,000	115,000	133,000	146,000	160,000	172,000
Government (AFGE)	106,000	139,000	200,000	295,000	325,000	293,000	300,000
Government (NAGE) (Ind.)	(5)	(5)	(5)	(5)	(5)	100,000	(5)
Graphic Arts[6]	—	—	—	—	—	106,000	100,000
Hotel	445,000	445,000	450,000	459,000	461,000	458,000	452,000
Iron	139,000	143,000	162,000	168,000	178,000	176,000	182,000
Laborers[7]	429,000	432,000	475,000	553,000	580,000	600,000	650,000
Ladies' Garment	441,000	442,000	455,000	455,000	442,000	428,000	405,000
Letter Carriers	150,000	168,000	190,000	210,000	215,000	220,000	232,000
Machinists	868,000	808,000	836,000	903,000	865,000	758,000	943,000
Maintenance of Way	153,000	121,000	141,000	125,000	126,000	142,000	119,000
Meat Cutters[8]	333,000	341,000	353,000	500,000	494,000	529,000	525,000
Mine, Mill (Ind.)[8]	75,000	75,000	—	—	—	—	—
Mine Workers (Ind.)	450,000	(5)	(5)	(5)	(5)	213,000	220,000
Musicians	282,000	275,000	252,000	283,000	300,000	315,000	330,000

Organization	1962	1964	1966	1968	1970	1972	1974
UNIONS							
Oil	168,000	162,000	165,000	173,000	175,000	172,000	177,000
Operating Engineers	297,000	311,000	330,000	350,000	393,000	402,000	415,000
Packinghouse[8]	98,000	145,000	135,000	—	—	—	—
Painters	196,000	199,000	201,000	200,000	210,000	208,000	211,000
Papermakers[10]	130,000	133,000	144,000	145,000	145,000	—	—
Paperworkers[10]	—	—	—	—	—	—	—
Plumbers	251,000	256,000	285,000	297,000	312,000	389,000[11]	301,000
Postal Clerks[12]	145,000	139,000	143,000	166,000	162,000	—	—
Postal Workers[12]	—	—	—	—	—	228,000	228,000[11]
Printing and Graphic[13]	—	—	—	—	—	239,000	249,000
Printing Pressmen[13]	116,000	116,000	114,000	126,000	128,000	—	129,000
Pulp[10]	174,000	176,000	171,000	183,000	193,000	115,000	—
Railroad Trainmen[14]	196,000	185,000	185,000	—	—	—	—
Railway Carmen	126,000	121,000	126,000	117,000	63,000[11]	104,000	96,000
Railway Clerks[15]	300,000	270,000	270,000	280,000	275,000	238,000	235,000
Retail Clerks	364,000	428,000	500,000	552,000	605,000	633,000	651,000
Retail, Wholesale	159,000	167,000	171,000	175,000	175,000	198,000	180,000
Rubber	158,000	165,000	170,000	204,000	216,000	183,000	191,000
Service Employees[16]	294,000	320,000	349,000	389,000	435,000	484,000	550,000
Sheet Metal	111,000	117,000	100,000	140,000	120,000[11]	153,000	161,000
State, County	220,000	235,000	281,000	364,000	444,000	529,000	648,000
Steelworkers[4]/[9]	879,000	965,000	1,068,000	1,120,000	1,200,000	1,400,000	1,300,000
Teachers	71,000	100,000	125,000	165,000	205,000	249,000	444,000
Teamsters (Ind.)	1,457,000	1,507,000	1,651,000	1,755,000	1,829,000	1,855,000	1,973,000
Textile Workers[3]	183,000	177,000	182,000	183,000	178,000	174,000	167,000
Transit Union[17]	134,000	133,000	103,000	134,000	132,000	130,000	140,000
Transport Workers	135,000	135,000	135,000	98,000	150,000	150,000	150,000
Transportation Union[14]	—	—	—	—	263,000	248,000	238,000
Typographical	106,000	113,000	107,000	123,000	112,000	115,000	111,000
Woodworkers	86,000	93,000	94,000	96,000	98,000	106,000	108,000

Figure 3 (Cont.)

Organization	1962	1964	1966	1968	1970	1972	1974
ASSOCIATIONS							
California	—	—	—	114,000	113,000	103,000	106,000
Civil Service (NYS)	—	—	—	175,000	190,000	202,000	207,000
Education Association	—	—	—	1,062,000	1,100,000	1,166,000	1,470,000
Nurses Association	—	—	—	204,000	181,000	157,000	196,000
Police	—	—	—	77,000	95,000	125,000	147,000

[1] Based on union reports to the Bureau for even-numbered years. All unions not identified as independent (Ind.) were affiliated with the AFL-CIO in 1974. Membership of employee associations was available only for years 1968 and after. Membership rounded to the nearest thousand.

[2] The American Bakery and Confectionery Workers' International Union and the Bakery and Confectionery Workers International Union of America merged on December 4, 1969.

[3] Merged with another labor organization in 1976. See appendix A for further information.

[4] Before the 1965 *Directory* District 50 appeared as a subordinate body of the United Mine Workers (Ind.), then changed its status from a District to an affiliated national union. In 1969, it became a separate national union. At its April 1970 convention, District 50 changed its name to the International Union of District 50, Allied and Technical Workers of the United States and Canada. On August 9, 1972, District 50 merged with the United Steelworkers of America (AFL-CIO).

[5] Membership not reported to the Bureau.

[6] On September 4, 1972, the International Brotherhood of Bookbinders (AFL-CIO) merged with the Lithographers and Photoengravers International Union (AFL-CIO) to form the Graphic Arts International Union (AFL-CIO). Combined membership is shown for 1972 and 1974.

[7] Prior to the 1965 *Directory* the Laborers were listed as the Hod Carriers, Building and Common Laborers' Union of America, International (AFL-CIO).

[8] On July 1, 1968, the United Packinghouse, Food and Allied Workers (AFL-CIO) merged with the Amalgamated Meat Cutters and Butcher Workmen of North America (AFL-CIO).

[9] The International Union of Mine, Mill and Smelter Workers (Ind.) merged with the United Steelworkers of America on July 1, 1967.

[10] On August 9, 1972, the United Papermakers and Paper workers (AFL-CIO) merged with the International Brotherhood of Pulp, Sulphite and Paper Mill Workers (AFL-CIO) to form the United Paperworkers International Union (AFL-CIO).

[11] AFL-CIO per capita reports.

[12] On July 1, 1971, the United Federation of Postal Clerks merged with four other Postal Service unions to form the American Postal Workers Union (AFL-CIO).

[13] On October 2, 1973, the International Union of Printing Pressmen and Assistants of North America (AFL-CIO) merged with the International Stereotypers', Electrotypers', and Platemakers' Union of North America (AFL-CIO) to form the International Printing and Graphic Communications Union (AFL-CIO).

[14] The Brotherhood of Railroad Trainmen (AFL-CIO) merged with three other unions on January 1, 1969 to form the United Transportation Union (AFL-CIO).

[15] Membership for years 1968 through 1974 includes the Transportation-Communication Employees Unions (AFL-CIO) which became a division in February 1969.

[16] In May 1968, the Building Service Employees International Union (AFL-CIO) changed its name to the Service Employees International Union (AFL-CIO).

[17] Prior to the 1965 *Directory*, the Transit Union was listed as Amalgamated Association of Street, Electrical Railway and Motor Coach Employees of America (AFL-CIO).

Figure 4. Distribution of membership of national unions and employee associations by economic sector, selected years, 1956-74

Year	Manufacturing		Nonmanufacturing		Government	
	Members (thousands)	Percent of all membership	Members (thousands)	Percent of all membership	Members (thousands)	Percent of all membership
Unions and associations:						
1968	9,218	41.9	8,940	40.6	3,857	17.5
1970	9,173	40.7	9,305	41.2	4,080	18.1
1972	8,920	38.7	9,619	41.7	4,520	19.6
1974	9,144	37.8	9,705	40.1	5,345	22.1
Unions:						
1956	8,839	48.8	8,350	46.1	915	5.1
1958	8,359	46.5	8,574	47.7	1,035	5.8
1960	8,591	47.6	8,375	46.4	1,070	5.9
1962	8,050	45.8	8,289	47.2	1,225	7.0
1964	8,342	46.6	8,125	45.3	1,453	8.1
1966	8,769	45.8	8,640	45.2	1,717	9.0
1968	9,218	45.6	8,837	43.7	2,155	10.7
1970	9,173	44.3	9,198	44.5	2,318	11.2
1972	8,920	42.8	9,458	45.4	2,460	11.8
1974	9,144	42.4	9,520	44.1	2,920	13.5

Figure 5. Distribution of national unions by number of basic collective bargaining agreements with employers, 1974[1]

Number of agreements	All unions		Agreements		AFL CIO		Unaffiliated	
	Number	Percent	Number	Percent	Unions	Agreements	Unions	Agreements
All unions[2]	172	100.0	194,726	100.0	108	146,589	64	48,137
No agreements[3]	4	2.3	—	—	—	—	4	—
Less than 25	53	30.8	344	.2	16	107	37	237
25 and under 100	25	14.5	1,336	.7	14	798	11	538
100 and under 200	23	13.4	3,126	1.6	19	2,591	4	535
200 and under 300	9	5.2	2,292	1.2	8	2,008	1	284
300 and under 500	11	6.4	4,234	2.2	8	3,231	3	1,003
500 and under 1,000	15	8.7	10,500	5.4	14	9,760	1	740
1,000 and under 2,000	15	8.7	18,889	9.7	14	17,389	1	1,500
2,000 and under 3,000	3	1.7	6,300	3.2	3	6,300	—	—
3,000 and under 5,000	5	2.9	17,750	9.1	4	14,450	1	3,300
5,000 and over	9	5.2	129,955	66.7	8	89,955	1	40,000

[1] The number of basic collective bargaining agreements does not include various supplements or pension, health, and welfare agreements as separate documents.

[2] Includes 36 unions for which the Bureau estimated the number of basic collective bargaining agreements. For 3 unions, the Hotel & Restaurant Employees and Bartenders International Union (AFL CIO), the Amalgamated Clothing Workers of America (AFL CIO) and the Pattern Makers League of North America (AFL CIO), sufficient information was not available on which to base an estimate.

[3] Though 4 unions report an absence of a collective bargaining agreement, this situation is a permanent characteristic of only the National Association of Postal Supervisors (Ind.) and the National League of Postmasters of the United States (Ind.) Both of these unions represent government employees. The National Hockey League Players' Association (Ind.) and the National Football League Players Association (Ind.) usually have such agreements but were without one at the time these data were collected.

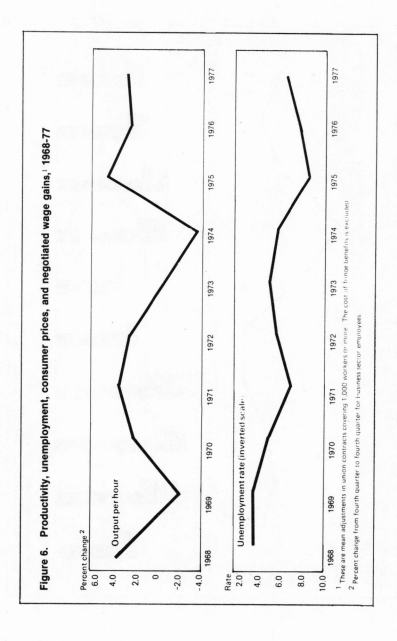

Figure 6. Productivity, unemployment, consumer prices, and negotiated wage gains,[1] 1968-77

Percent change [2]

6.0 4.0 2.0 0 -2.0 -4.0

Output per hour

1968 1969 1970 1971 1972 1973 1974 1975 1976 1977

Rate

2.0 4.0 6.0 8.0 10.0

Unemployment rate (inverted scale)

1968 1969 1970 1971 1972 1973 1974 1975 1976 1977

[1] These are mean adjustments in union contracts covering 1,000 workers or more. The cost of fringe benefits is excluded.
[2] Percent change from fourth quarter to fourth quarter for business sector employees.

Figure 6 (Cont.)

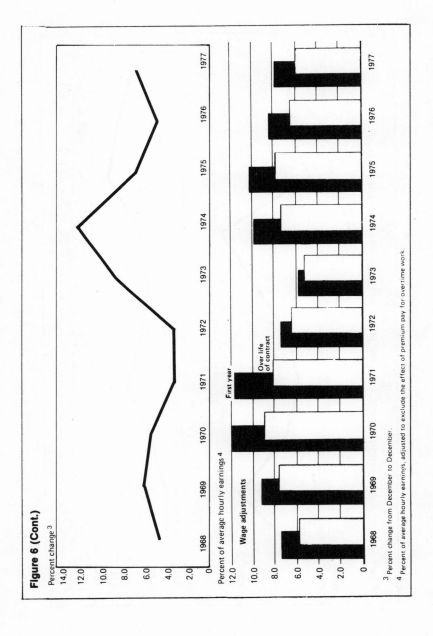

Percent change [3]

Percent of average hourly earnings [4]

[3] Percent change from December to December.

[4] Percent of average hourly earnings, adjusted to exclude the effect of premium pay for overtime work.

Figure 7. Indexes of Output Per Hour of All Persons and Related Data, Private Economy,¹ 1967-75

[1967=100]

Year	Output per hour of all persons				Output per employed person				Output				Employment				Hours			
	Total private	Farm	Non farm	Manufacturing	Total private	Farm	Non farm	Manufacturing	Total private	Farm	Non farm	Manufacturing	Total private	Farm	Non farm	Manufacturing	Total private	Farm	Non farm	Manufacturing
Hour estimates based primarily on establishment data																				
1967	100.0	100.0	100.0	100.0	100.0	100.0	100.0	100.0	100.0	100.0	100.0	100.0	100.0	100.0	100.0	100.0	100.0	100.0	100.0	100.0
1968	102.7	101.5	102.6	103.6	102.3	102.2	102.2	103.9	104.5	99.3	104.7	105.6	102.2	97.2	102.5	101.7	101.7	97.8	102.0	102.0
1969	102.7	108.5	102.2	105.0	101.7	109.0	101.4	105.0	107.2	101.0	107.5	108.7	105.2	92.7	106.0	103.6	104.4	93.1	105.2	103.6
1970	103.9	121.1	102.8	104.5	101.7	119.9	100.8	103.0	106.8	101.0	106.9	102.6	105.0	87.6	106.1	99.6	102.8	86.7	104.0	98.2
1971	105.7	131.6	106.4	110.2	105.0	130.8	103.8	108.8	110.2	110.8	110.2	103.9	105.0	84.7	106.2	95.6	102.4	84.2	103.6	94.3
1972	107.7	127.0	110.0	115.7	108.6	125.0	107.6	115.6	117.4	108.1	117.7	113.7	108.1	86.5	109.4	98.3	105.6	85.1	107.0	98.2
1973	113.7	134.7	112.2	117.8	110.8	131.9	109.6	117.9	124.3	112.2	124.7	121.8	112.2	85.1	113.8	103.3	109.3	83.3	111.1	103.4
1974	110.8	127.6	109.5	113.1	106.8	121.4	105.8	111.8	121.5	106.4	122.0	115.4	113.8	85.9	115.4	103.2	109.6	83.4	111.5	102.0
1975	112.2	146.7	110.5	112.4	107.2	144.2	105.6	110.0	118.5	118.7	118.5	104.1	110.5	82.3	112.2	94.6	105.5	81.0	110.2	92.6
RATES OF CHANGE 1968-75	1.6	4.4	1.4	1.6	1.0	4.0	.9	1.4	2.4	2.0	2.4	1.0	1.4	-1.9	1.6	-.5	.9	-2.3	1.0	-.7
Hour estimates based primarily on labor force data																				
1967	100.0	100.0	100.0		100.0	100.0	100.0		100.0	100.0	100.0		100.0	100.0	100.0		100.0	100.0	100.0	
1968	103.7	101.8	103.6		103.7	101.1	103.3		104.5	99.3	104.7		101.2	98.3	101.3		100.8	97.5	101.0	
1969	104.6	107.0	104.0		103.7	107.1	103.2		107.2	101.0	107.5		103.4	92.2	104.1		102.6	91.3	103.4	
1970	106.1	125.9	104.9		103.0	120.2	102.0		106.8	105.1	106.9		103.8	87.4	104.8		100.7	83.5	101.9	
1971	109.7	134.9	108.3		105.8	129.1	104.6		110.0	110.8	110.2		104.2	85.8	105.4		100.5	82.2	101.8	
1972	113.2	130.6	111.9		109.3	123.7	108.4		117.4	108.1	117.7		107.4	87.4	108.6		103.7	82.8	105.2	
1973	115.6	137.9	114.0		111.7	130.1	110.5		124.3	112.2	124.7		111.2	86.2	112.8		107.5	81.3	109.4	
1974	111.1	129.6	109.6		107.9	121.4	106.9		121.5	106.4	122.0		112.6	87.7	114.2		109.4	82.1	114.4	
1975	113.1	151.0	111.2		108.9	142.3	107.3		118.5	118.6	118.5		108.8	83.3	110.5		104.7	78.5	106.6	
RATES OF CHANGE 1968-75	1.4	4.6	1.2		1.0	3.8	.9		2.4	2.0	2.4		1.4	-1.7	1.6		1.0	-2.5	1.2	

¹Output refers to gross domestic product in 1972 dollars. Employment includes self employed and unpaid family workers as well as wage and salary workers.

Figure 8. Gross National Product in Constant Dollars, 1967-76

[Billions of 1972 dollars]

Item	1967	1968	1969	1970	1971	1972	1973	1974¹	1975¹	1976¹
Gross national product	1,007.7	1,051.8	1,078.8	1,075.3	1,107.5	1,171.1	1,235.0	1,214.0	1,191.7	1,264.7
Personal consumption expenditures	603.2	633.4	655.4	668.9	691.9	733.0	767.7	759.1	770.3	813.7
Durable goods	79.7	88.2	91.9	88.9	98.1	111.2	121.8	112.3	111.9	125.8
Nondurable goods	259.5	270.2	276.4	282.7	287.5	299.3	309.3	303.5	306.1	319.3
Services	264.0	275.0	287.2	297.3	306.3	322.4	336.5	343.4	352.4	368.6
Gross private domestic investment	152.7	159.5	168.0	154.7	166.8	188.3	207.2	182.0	137.8	170.9
Fixed investment	140.7	150.8	157.5	150.4	160.2	178.8	190.7	173.5	149.8	162.8
Nonresidential	103.5	108.0	114.3	110.0	108.0	116.8	131.0	128.5	114.4	115.7
Structures	41.1	42.0	44.0	42.8	41.7	42.5	45.5	42.1	36.7	38.1
Producers durable equipment	62.4	66.1	70.3	67.2	66.3	74.3	85.5	86.5	74.7	77.7
Residential	37.2	42.8	43.2	40.4	52.2	62.0	59.7	45.0	38.4	47.1
Nonfarm structures	35.5	41.1	41.5	38.9	50.5	60.3	57.9	42.9	36.6	45.1
Farm structures	.9	.8	.9	.6	.7	.7	.5	.8	.6	.7
Producers durable equipment	.8	.9	.9	.9	1.0	1.1	1.2	1.3	1.2	1.3
Change in business inventories	12.0	8.7	10.6	4.3	6.6	9.4	16.5	8.5	-12.0	8.1
Nonfarm	11.2	8.5	10.3	3.9	5.2	8.8	14.2	8.9	-13.0	8.1
Farm	.8	.2	.3	.4	1.5	.6	2.3	.4	.9	.0
Net exports of goods and services	3.5	.4	1.3	1.4	.6	3.3	7.6	16.5	22.6	16.0
Exports	54.2	58.5	62.2	67.1	67.9	72.7	87.4	97.2	90.6	96.1
Imports	50.7	58.9	63.5	65.7	68.5	75.9	79.9	80.7	68.1	80.1
Government purchases of goods and services	248.3	259.2	256.7	250.2	249.4	253.1	252.5	256.4	261.0	264.1
Federal	125.3	128.3	121.8	110.7	103.9	102.1	96.9	95.3	95.7	96.7
State and local	123.1	130.9	134.9	139.5	145.5	151.0	155.9	161.1	165.2	167.4

¹Preliminary. Each year data for the previous 3 years are revised

143

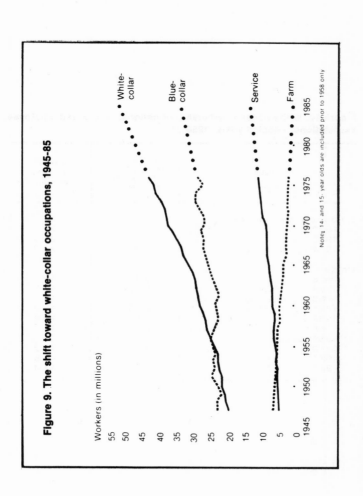

Figure 9. The shift toward white-collar occupations, 1945-85

Workers (in millions)

Note: 14- and 15- year olds are included prior to 1958 only

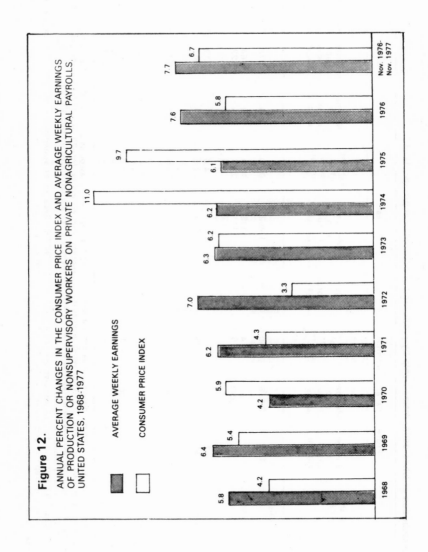

Figure 12.

ANNUAL PERCENT CHANGES IN THE CONSUMER PRICE INDEX AND AVERAGE WEEKLY EARNINGS OF PRODUCTION OR NONSUPERVISORY WORKERS ON PRIVATE NONAGRICULTURAL PAYROLLS. UNITED STATES. 1968-1977

Figure 13. General Wage Changes in Major Collective Bargaining Situations[1] 1967-75

Year	All industries studied				Manufacturing				Nonmanufacturing			
	Median adjustment		Median increase		Median adjustment		Median increase		Median adjustment		Median increase	
	Cents	Percent	Cents	Percent	Cents	Percent	Cents	Percent	Cents	Percent	Cents	Percent
First year changes in contracts negotiated during year												
1967	16.0	5.6	16.1	5.7	17.5	6.4	18.0	6.4	15.0	5.0	15.0	5.0
1968	23.5	7.2	23.5	7.2	23.5	6.9	23.5	6.9	23.6	7.5	23.6	7.5
1969	25.0	8.0	25.0	8.0	21.4	7.0	21.5	7.0	36.8	10.0	36.8	10.0
1970	32.9	10.0	32.9	10.0	26.3	7.5	26.3	7.5	56.0	14.2	56.0	14.2
1971	44.1	12.2	44.1	12.5	38.4	10.0	39.0	10.1	44.1	12.8	44.1	13.0
1972	28.0	6.3	28.0	6.6	23.3	6.2	24.0	6.2	31.6	6.6	32.3	6.6
1973	26.4	5.5	26.4	5.5	26.4	5.6	26.4	5.6	30.0	5.5	30.0	5.5
1974	45.0	9.0	45.0	9.0	40.0	7.7	40.0	7.7	51.3	9.2	52.0	9.3
1975	61.7	10.0	65.0	10.0	42.0	9.0	45.0	9.2	70.0	10.0	70.0	10.2
Annual rate of change over life of contracts negotiated during year												
1967	14.7	5.0	14.7	5.0	14.5	5.1	14.5	5.1	14.7	5.0	14.7	5.0
1968	17.2	5.2	17.2	5.2	17.0	4.9	17.0	4.9	20.1	5.9	20.1	5.9
1969	21.2	6.8	21.2	6.8	15.8	5.8	15.8	5.8	32.6	8.5	32.6	8.5
1970	31.4	8.1	31.4	8.1	19.0	5.8	19.0	5.8	47.3	12.1	47.3	12.1
1971	31.7	8.0	31.9	8.0	27.6	7.4	28.0	7.5	33.8	8.4	38.9	8.5
1972	25.4	6.0	25.6	6.0	21.0	5.6	21.1	5.6	30.7	6.6	31.6	6.7
1973	23.3	5.2	23.3	5.2	20.6	5.0	20.6	5.0	31.4	5.5	31.7	5.5
1974	33.6	6.6	33.6	6.6	27.9	5.3	27.9	5.3	41.7	7.7	41.8	7.7
1975	47.2	7.4	49.1	7.4	33.6	7.4	34.5	7.5	52.2	7.4	52.2	7.4
Changes effective in year												
1967	12.9	4.4	15.0	4.8	12.0	4.0	12.0	4.4	14.9	4.8	18.0	5.2
1968	19.0	5.5	19.2	5.7	18.2	5.2	19.0	5.4	20.0	6.0	21.8	6.5
1969	19.0	5.1	19.1	5.1	17.5	5.0	18.0	5.0	20.0	5.2	20.0	5.6
1970	25.4	7.3	27.5	7.8	20.0	6.0	20.6	6.0	37.5	8.3	42.5	9.7
1971	31.3	8.0	37.8	9.2	25.3	6.3	27.1	6.6	44.1	10.7	45.1	12.1
1972	25.6	6.0	26.0	6.4	23.0	5.2	23.0	5.4	30.4	7.2	40.1	7.6
1973	34.3	7.3	35.5	7.4	30.0	7.3	30.2	7.4	36.2	7.2	36.2	7.5
1974	43.3	9.5	45.0	9.6	46.0	11.1	46.8	11.3	42.5	8.0	42.5	8.2
1975	53.7	8.6	53.7	8.6	53.3	8.6	53.7	8.6	55.2	8.6	55.2	8.8

[1]Defined as those involving 1,000 workers or more

Figure 14. Average Percent Change In Hourly Cost of Wages and Benefits Negotiated in Collective Bargaining Settlements Covering 5,000 Workers or More, 1967-75

Year	All industries studied		Manufacturing		Nonmanufacturing	
	Mean adjustment	Median adjustment	Mean adjustment	Median adjustment	Mean adjustment	Median adjustment
First year changes in contracts negotiated during year						
1967	7.4	7.3	8.4	9.0	6.5	4.9
1968	8.7	8.1	8.7	8.1	8.6	8.2
1969	10.9	10.9	9.6	8.8	12.3	11.8
1970	13.1	12.0	9.9	8.8	15.9	14.0
1971	13.1	13.9	11.7	13.5	14.1	16.0
1972	8.5	7.9	8.5	8.2	8.5	7.9
1973	7.1	6.8	7.0	5.9	7.1	7.0
1974	10.7	10.5	8.8	7.0	11.6	10.5
1975	11.4	11.4	10.4	11.3	11.6	11.9
Annual rate of change over life of contracts negotiated during year						
1967	5.1	5.2	5.1	5.2	5.2	4.8
1968	6.5	6.0	5.9	5.9	7.1	6.5
1969	8.2	7.4	6.6	6.6	9.7	9.6
1970	9.1	8.4	6.2	5.5	11.5	11.7
1971	8.8	9.0	7.7	8.8	9.5	9.0
1972	7.4	6.9	6.3	6.2	7.9	7.9
1973	6.1	5.5	6.0	5.5	6.2	6.1
1974	7.8	6.5	6.7	6.2	8.3	7.2
1975	8.1	7.8	9.2	11.3	7.8	7.8
Changes effective in year						
1968	6.8	6.4	6.3	6.3	7.1	7.1
1969	6.5	5.7	5.7	5.0	7.4	6.2
1970	9.0	8.7	7.7	6.3	10.1	10.6
1971	9.8	8.5	8.2	8.5	11.1	11.6
1972	7.6	6.7	6.2	5.7	8.7	8.0
1973	7.9	7.8	8.0	7.8	7.9	8.5
1974	10.4	10.5	12.1	13.2	9.2	8.1
1975	9.4	8.4	9.0	8.0	9.3	9.4

Figure 15. Highlights of wage and benefit changes, 1973-77

Coverage and measure	Average percent adjustment				
	1973	1974	1975	1976	1977
Settlements affecting 1,000 workers or more:					
First-year wage-rate adjustment	5.8	9.8	10.2	8.4	7.8
Excluding construction	6.0	9.5	11.1	8.8	8.2
Nonmanufacturing	5.7	10.5	10.4	7.7	7.4
Excluding construction	6.0	10.2	11.9	8.6	8.0
Average annual wage-rate adjustment over life of contract	5.1	7.3	7.8	6.4	5.8
Excluding construction	5.3	6.7	8.0	6.5	5.7
Nonmanufacturing	5.3	8.0	7.8	6.8	6.0
Excluding construction	5.4	7.2	8.0	7.2	5.9
Major collective bargaining units of 1,000 workers or more:					
Effective wage-rate adjustment:					
Total	7.0	9.4	8.7	8.1	8.0
Adjustment resulting from:					
Current settlement	3.0	4.8	2.8	3.2	3.0
Prior settlement	2.7	2.6	3.7	3.2	3.2
Escalator provision	1.3	1.9	2.2	1.6	1.7
Settlements affecting 5,000 workers or more:					
First-year wage-rate adjustment	5.7	9.9	10.5	8.3	7.9
First-year adjustment in wages and benefits combined	7.1	10.7	11.4	8.5	9.6
Excluding construction	7.2	10.5	12.7	8.7	10.1
Nonmanufacturing	7.1	11.6	11.6	8.3	9.4
Excluding construction	7.5	11.6	13.4	8.7	10.3
Average annual wage-rate adjustment over life of contract ..	4.9	7.0	7.6	6.1	5.5
Average annual wages and benefits combined over life of contract ..	6.1	7.8	8.1	6.6	6.2
Excluding construction	6.2	7.4	8.4	6.6	6.2
Nonmanufacturing	6.2	8.3	7.8	7.2	6.5
Excluding construction	6.4	7.8	8.2	7.4	6.5

Figure 16. Average Hourly Earnings of Production or Nonsupervisory Workers on Private Nonagricultural Payrolls, by Industry Division, 1967-76

Year and month	Total private	Mining	Contract construction	Manufacturing			Manufacturing excluding overtime	Transportation and public utilities	Wholesale and retail trade			Finance, insurance and real estate	Services
				Total	Durable goods	Nondurable goods			Total	Wholesale	Retail		
1967	$2.68	$3.19	$4.11	$2.83	$3.00	$2.57	$2.72	$3.24	$2.24	$2.88	$2.01	$2.58	$2.29
1968	2.85	3.35	4.41	3.01	3.19	2.74	2.88	3.42	2.40	3.05	2.16	2.75	2.42
1969	3.04	3.61	4.79	3.19	3.38	2.91	3.06	3.64	2.55	3.23	2.30	2.93	2.61
1970	3.22	3.85	5.24	3.36	3.55	3.08	3.24	3.85	2.71	3.44	2.44	3.08	2.81
1971	3.44	4.06	5.69	3.57	3.79	3.26	3.44	4.21	2.86	3.67	2.57	3.27	3.02
1972	3.67	4.41	6.03	3.81	4.06	3.47	3.66	4.64	3.01	3.88	2.70	3.42	3.23
1973	3.92	4.73	6.37	4.08	4.34	3.68	3.89	5.04	3.20	4.12	2.87	3.58	3.46
1974	4.22	5.21	6.75	4.41	4.69	3.99	4.24	5.43	3.47	4.49	3.09	3.82	3.76
1975	4.54	5.90	7.25	4.81	5.14	4.35	4.66	5.92	3.75	4.89	3.34	4.13	4.06
1976	4.87	6.42	7.68	5.19	5.55	4.68	5.00	6.46	3.97	5.18	3.55	4.36	4.36

Figure 17. The Consumer Price Index and Major Groups, 1967-76

(1967=100)

Period	All items	Food	Housing	Apparel and upkeep	Transportation	Medical care	Personal care	Reading and recreation	Other goods and services
1967	100.0	100.0	100.0	100.0	100.0	100.0	100.0	100.0	100.0
1968	104.2	103.6	104.2	105.4	103.2	106.1	104.2	104.7	104.6
1969	109.8	108.9	110.8	111.5	107.2	113.4	109.3	108.7	109.1
1970	116.3	114.9	118.9	116.1	112.7	120.6	113.2	113.4	116.0
1971	121.3	118.4	124.3	119.8	118.6	128.4	116.8	119.3	120.9
1972	125.3	123.5	129.2	122.3	119.9	132.5	119.8	122.8	125.5
1973	133.1	141.4	135.0	126.8	123.8	137.7	125.2	125.9	129.0
1974	147.7	161.7	150.6	136.2	137.7	150.5	137.3	133.8	137.2
1975	161.2	175.4	166.8	142.3	150.6	168.6	150.7	144.4	147.4
1976	170.5	180.8	177.2	147.6	165.5	184.7	160.5	151.2	153.3

Figure 20. Comparison of percent increase in salaries under the General Schedule and earnings for selected occupational groups

Occupational group	Annual rate of increase from July 1962 to:					
	April 1972	April 1973	April 1974	April 1975	April 1976	April 1977
Government						
Federal employees under the General Schedule:						
Basic annual salary scales	5.8	5.8	5.7	5.6	5.5	5.5
Average annual salary rates	6.1	6.0	5.9	5.8	5.8	5.8
Average annual salaries	7.4	7.2	6.9	6.8	6.8	6.7
Private industry						
Professional, administrative, technical, and clerical employees, average salaries:						
Clerical and beginning technicians	4.2	4.5	4.6	5.0	5.2	5.2
Entry and development professional working levels, advanced technical levels, and supervisors of nonprofessional levels	4.7	4.8	4.9	5.1	5.2	5.3
Fully experienced professional working levels, supervisors of professional levels, and program administrative levels	4.7	4.9	5.0	5.3	5.4	5.5
Production and nonsupervisory workers in private nonfarm economy, average hourly earnings adjusted for overtime (in manufacturing only) and interindustry employment shifts	5.2	5.5	5.3	5.7	6.0	6.1

Figure 21. Indexes of Salaries[1] of Federal Employees in the United States Covered by the General Schedule, 1967-76

[October 1967 = 100]

Date	Basic salary scales[1]	Average salary rates[1]	Average salaries[1]
October 1, 1967[2]	100.0	100.0	100.0
July 1, 1968[2]	104.9	104.9	106.5
July 1, 1969[2]	114.4	114.9	120.0
July 1, 1970	121.3	122.3	130.0
July 1, 1971	128.6	130.0	139.2
April 1, 1972[3]	135.6	138.0	148.2
April 1, 1973	142.6	145.1	156.0
April 1, 1974	149.4	151.6	162.0
April 1, 1975	157.5	159.3	171.1
April 1, 1976	165.4	167.1	181.7
October 1, 1976[4]	173.8		

[1]Basic salary scales reflect only statutory changes in salaries. Average salary rates show statutory changes and the effect of changes in the proportion of workers at each step within the salary ranges for individual grades. Average salaries measure the effect of these two types of change, as well as change in the proportion of workers in the various grades.

[2]Indexes include increases effective the first pay period beginning in the month.

[3]In 1972, the reference date was changed to April 1, from July 1, because of a change in the Civil Service Commission's reference date for employment figures which are used as weights in the index calculations.

[4]Effective date of the 1976 salary increase.

Figure 22. Indexes of Annual Maximum Salary Scales of Firefighters and Police in Cities of 100,000 or More, 1967-76

[1967 = 100]

Year	Fire-fighters and police	Fire-fighters	Police
1967	100	100	100
1968	107	107	107
1969	117	118	118
1970	128	128	128
1971	135	136	135
1972	145	145	145
1973	157	157	158
1974	167	167	168
1975	180	181	180
1976 p	193	193	192

ppreliminary

Figure 23. Indexes of Average Annual Salaries of Urban Public Classroom Teachers, by Size of City and County,[1] 1967-76

[1967=100]

School year ending in June	All systems	1,000,000 or more	500,000 and under 1,000,000	250,000 and under 500,000	100,000 and under 250,000
1967	100	100	100	100	100
1969	114	111	115	115	116
1971	131	127	131	133	133
1973	149	152	145	148	148
1975	171	176	168	169	170
1976	184	188	180	183	182

[1]Data refer to cities with 100,000 inhabitants or more in 1970, and to counties of this size (in SMSA'S) that had county-wide school districts.

NOTE: In computing average salaries and increases, all teachers in each system were classified according to the average salary in that system. The effect of period-to-period employment changes in calculating percentage changes in average salaries was minimized by using constant weights (employment in the last year of each pair of years).

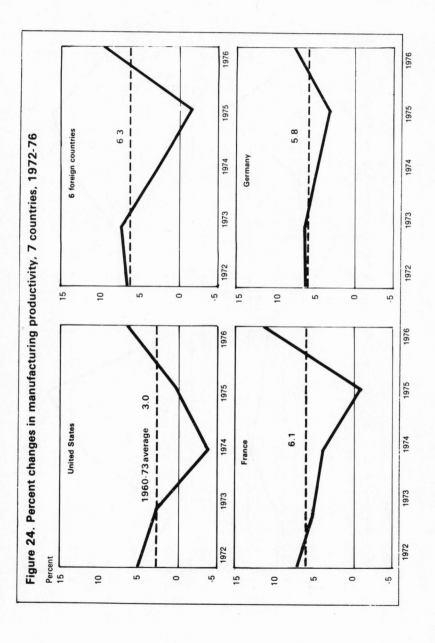

Figure 24. Percent changes in manufacturing productivity, 7 countries, 1972-76

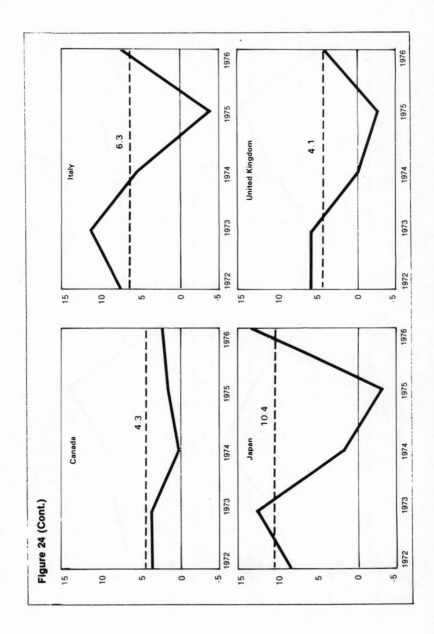

Figure 24 (Cont.)

Figure 25. Unemployment in Selected Industrial Countries, 1967-76

Year	Adjusted to U.S. concepts									As published [2]					
	United States [1]	Australia [1]	Canada [1]	France	Germany, F.R. and West Berlin	Great Britain	Italy	Japan	Sweden	France	Germany, F.R. and West Berlin	Great Britain	Italy	Japan	Sweden
	Unemployment rate [4], [5]														
1967	3.8	1.6	3.8	2.1	1.3	3.4	3.8	1.3	2.1	1.8	2.1	2.2	3.5	1.3	2.1
1968	3.6	1.5	4.5	2.8	1.6	3.3	3.9	1.2	2.2	2.1	1.5	2.4	3.5	1.2	2.2
1969	3.5	1.5	4.4	2.6	.9	3.0	3.7	1.1	1.9	1.7	.9	2.4	3.4	1.1	1.9
1970	4.9	1.4	5.7	2.8	.8	3.1	3.5	1.2	1.5	1.7	.7	2.5	3.2	1.2	1.5
1971	5.9	1.6	6.2	3.0	.8	3.9	3.5	1.3	2.6	2.1	.8	3.4	3.2	1.2	2.5
1972	5.6	2.2	6.2	3.0	.8	4.2	4.0	1.4	2.7	2.3	1.1	3.7	3.7	1.4	2.7
1973	4.9	1.9	5.6	2.9	.8	3.2	3.8	1.3	2.5	2.1	1.2	2.6	3.5	1.3	2.5
1974	5.6	2.3	5.4	3.1	1.7	3.2	3.2	1.4	2.0	2.3	2.6	2.6	2.9	1.4	2.0
1975	8.5	4.4	6.9	4.3	3.8	4.7	3.7	1.9	1.6	4.1	4.8	4.1	3.3	1.9	1.6
1976	7.7	4.4	7.1	4.6	4.0	6.4	4.0	2.0	1.6	4.6	4.6	5.6	3.7	2.0	1.6

[1] Published and adjusted data for the United States, Australia, and Canada are identical.

[2] Published figures for Germany, Italy, Japan, and Sweden include military personnel.

[3] Preliminary estimates based on incomplete data.

[4] Published figures for the United States, Australia, Canada, Italy, Japan, and Sweden refer to unemployment as recorded by sample labor force surveys; for France, to annual estimates of unemployment; and for Germany and Great Britain to the registered unemployed.

[5] Adjusted figures: as a percent of the civilian labor force. Published figures: for France, unemployment as a percent of the civilian labor force; for Italy, Japan, and Sweden, unemployment as a percent of the civilian labor force plus career military personnel; for Germany and Great Britain, registered unemployed as a percent of employed wage and salary workers plus the unemployed. With the excep-

tion of France, which does not publish an unemployment rate, these are the usually published rates for each country. Published rates shown for Germany and Great Britain cannot be computed from the data contained in this table.

NOTE: The adjusted statistics, insofar as possible have been adapted to the age at which compulsory schooling ends in each country. Therefore, the data for the United States and the adjusted data for France, Sweden, and beginning in 1973, Great Britain relate to the population 16 years of age and over; the data for Australia, Canada, Germany, Japan, and, prior to 1973, Great Britain relate to the population 15 years of age and over; and the data for Italy relate to the population 14 years of age and over.

Figure 26. Indexes of Output Per Hour and Unit Labor Costs in Manufacturing,[1] Selected Countries, 1967-75

(1967 = 100)

Item and country	1967	1968	1969	1970	1971	1972	1973	1974	1975
Output per hour:									
United States	100.0	103.6	104.9	104.5	110.3	116.0	119.4	114.7	114.9
Belgium	100.0	109.2	118.8	129.5	136.9	153.2	166.7	175.2	190.0
Canada	100.0	107.3	113.3	115.2	122.9	127.4	132.2	132.3	134.4
Denmark	100.0	109.8	120.3	129.?	138.8	150.7	159.8	166.9	177.3
France	100.0	114.4	115.4	121.2	127.8	137.0	144.1	149.8	148.9
Germany, F R and West Berlin	100.0	107.6	113.8	116.6	122.5	130.3	138.6	145.6	150.4
Italy	100.0	108.4	112.2	117.8	123.5	132.9	147.8	155.6	151.0
Japan	100.0	112.6	130.0	146.5	151.7	163.9	184.3	187.5	181.7
Netherlands	100.0	112.7	122.6	134.4	143.4	154.8	168.4	178.9	174.7
Sweden	100.0	110.1	118.3	124.5	129.0	137.9	147.4	152.1	152.8
United Kingdom	100.0	107.1	108.4	109.1	114.5	121.1	128.2	127.9	124.3
Switzerland	100.0	105.2	116.1	125.5	131.3	137.9	147.7	150.7	144.8
Unit labor cost in U S dollars:[2]									
United States	100.0	103.3	108.7	11?.?	117.6	118.1	123.2	140.9	156.4
Belgium	100.0	96.9	97.1	101.4	112.3	128.6	153.6	178.2	212.7
Canada	100.0	100.1	101.9	115.5	115.7	121.9	126.6	145.4	160.3
Denmark	100.0	101.5	95.8	104.4	106.8	117.3	147.5	168.4	201.6
France	100.0	101.1	98.8	98.9	105.2	119.9	146.3	158.0	210.4
Germany, F R and West Berlin	100.0	98.3	103.1	124.6	141.8	162.5	208.3	235.3	267.5
Italy	100.0	99.0	104.3	119.2	135.6	152.2	177.5	183.4	243.2
Japan	100.0	103.8	107.2	113.3	130.7	160.1	194.3	233.4	272.0
Netherlands	100.0	99.1	102.7	108.4	120.3	138.8	175.8	203.4	256.0
Sweden	100.0	99.5	100.?	105.1	115.8	132.8	148.5	165.9	216.3
United Kingdom	100.0	87.1	92.8	106.0	117.8	126.7	134.1	15?.2	199.0
Switzerland	100.0	100.3	97.1	99.7	113.1	129.5	165.2	194.9	?50.2

[1]The data relate to all employed persons in the United States and Canada wage earners only in Switzerland, and all employees in other countries

[2]Indexes in national currency adjusted for changes in exchange rates

Figure 27. Estimated Compensation Per Hour Worked of Production Workers in Manufacturing, Selected Countries, 1967-76.

Item and country	1967	1968	1969	1970	1971	1972	1973	1974	1975	1976[1]
Total compensation per hour worked in U.S. dollars:[2]										
United States	3.44	3.68	3.93	4.19	4.49	4.82	5.24	5.73	6.32	6.84
Belgium	1.57	1.66	1.82	2.08	2.46	3.18	4.22	5.13	6.62	7.09
Canada	2.63	2.85	3.09	3.45	3.91	4.33	4.69	5.49	6.16	7.32
France	1.42	1.56	1.63	1.73	1.94	2.37	3.08	3.41	4.52	4.65
Germany	1.60	1.67	1.89	2.33	2.78	3.36	4.58	5.40	6.26	6.62
Italy	1.19	1.25	1.38	1.68	2.01	2.42	2.99	3.45	4.42	4.22
Japan	.60	.71	.84	.99	1.18	1.58	2.19	2.67	3.05	3.29
Netherlands	1.53	1.68	1.89	2.14	2.58	3.16	4.29	5.31	6.48	6.74
Sweden	2.21	2.36	2.60	2.96	3.26	4.02	4.95	5.66	7.20	8.27
United Kingdom	1.26	1.18	1.29	1.48	1.73	2.03	2.28	2.59	3.21	3.04

[1]Preliminary.

[2]Total compensation includes all direct payments made to the worker (pay for time worked, pay for vacations, holidays, and other leave, all bonuses, and pay in kind) before payroll deductions of any kind, plus employer expenditures for legally-required insurance programs and contractual and private plans for the benefit of employees. In addition, compensation includes other significant taxes on payrolls or employment that are regarded as labor costs.

Figure 28. Annual percent change in manufacturing productivity and output, 12 countries, 1960-76

Country	Output per hour						Output					
	1960-73[1]	1974	1975	1976	1976[3] 1st half	2d half	1960-73[1]	1974	1975	1976	1976[2] 1st half	2d half
United States	3.0	3.9	0.2	6.5	10.1	4.8	4.5	-5.2	-9.0	11.2	15.8	8.8
Canada	4.3	.1	1.5	2.4	2.7	2.1	6.2	3.0	-4.9	4.8	4.8	4.9
Japan	10.4	1.7	-3.1	12.9	12.3	13.6	12.6	-3.1	-11.1	13.7	13.5	13.8
France	6.1	4.0	-.6	11.5	11.1	12.2	6.6	3.7	-4.9	10.2	8.6	12.1
Germany	5.8	6.3	3.8	8.2	9.6	6.8	5.6	.5	-6.1	9.0	9.7	8.5
Italy	6.3	5.4	-3.6	7.5	-----	-----	6.8	6.4	-9.7	12.4	-----	-----
United Kingdom....	4.1	-.2	-2.8	4.0	4.5	3.6	3.1	-2.5	-5.9	1.6	-.5	3.9
Six foreign countries..	6.3	3.5	-.6	9.2	-----	-----	6.9	.4	-7.4	9.6	-----	-----
Belgium	7.0	7.3	5.5	-----	12.3	[3]8.8	6.5	3.3	-6.5	10.4	9.0	11.8
Denmark	7.2	4.5	6.2	10.8	13.1	8.4	6.2	3.0	-7.0	11.0	13.0	9.0
Netherlands	7.6	6.7	-2.3	-----	9.5	[3]12.3	6.4	2.6	-6.8	6.0	5.2	7.0
Sweden	7.0	3.1	.5	.3	-.8	1.6	5.5	4.4	-1.1	-2.5	-4.1	-.8
Switzerland........	5.2	2.0	-3.9	8.6	14.2	3.1	4.7	1.3	-14.5	1.6	2.7	.5
Eleven foreign countries........	6.3	3.7	-.5	-----	-----	-----	6.7	.7	-7.4	-----	-----	-----
Nine European countries........	5.9	4.3	-.1	-----	-----	-----	5.5	1.8	-6.4	-----	-----	-----

[1] Percent changes computed from the least squares trend of the logarithms of the index numbers.
[2] Percent change over same period of 1975.
[3] Third quarter.
NOTE: Dashes indicate data not available.

Figure 29. Annual percent change in manufacturing hourly compensation, 12 countries, 1960-76

Country	1960–73[1]	1974	1975	1976	1976[2]	
					1st half	2d half
United States	5.1	9.9	11.2	7.5	7.1	7.9
Canada.	6.3	12.4	16.4	11.5	11.8	11.1
Japan	14.6	31.5	15.0	8.8	8.6	9.0
France	9.5	18.6	18.5	13.0	11.7	13.8
Germany	9.6	15.7	11.6	5.3	4.1	6.4
Italy	11.7	25.2	30.0	18.4	- - - - - -	- - - - - -
United Kingdom.	8.4	22.5	29.6	16.2	20.1	12.4
Six foreign countries. . . .	9.9	21.5	18.0	11.2	- - - - - -	- - - - - -
Belgium.	10.7	22.5	23.2	12.2	13.4	11.2
Denmark	11.4	20.4	19.9	11.3	11.6	11.0
Netherlands	12.8	18.8	15.5	8.8	10.5	7.2
Sweden.	10.3	17.3	22.4	20.6	26.0	15.9
Switzerland	8.6	13.2	7.3	1.6	1.6	1.6
Eleven foreign countries .	9.9	21.1	17.9	- - - - - -	- - - - - -	- - - - - -
Nine European countries .	9.8	18.6	18.6	- - - - - -	- - - - - -	- - - - - -

[1] Percent changes computed from the least squares trend of the logarithms of the index numbers.
[2] Percent change over same period of 1975

NOTE: Dashes indicate data not available.

**Figure 30. Two-tier Patterns of Unemployment
Indexes of Seasonally Adjusted Unemployment Rates
May 1975 = 100**

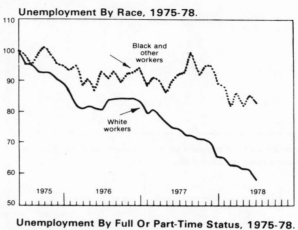

Unemployment By Race, 1975-78.

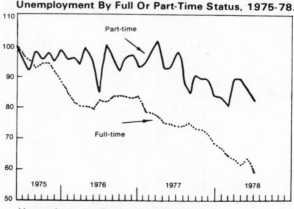

Unemployment By Full Or Part-Time Status, 1975-78.

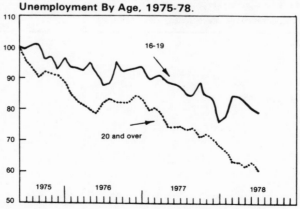

Unemployment By Age, 1975-78.

Figure 31. The Diversity of Unemployment in the United States, Second Quarter, 1978

Category	Value
White males, 20 and over	3.5
All males, 20 and over	4.0
Veterans, 20-34	4.3
White females, 20 and over	5.0
All whites, 16 and over	5.0
All persons, 16 and over in non-poverty areas	5.3
All females, 20 and over	5.7
All persons, 20 and over	5.8
Spanish origin males, 20 and over	5.8
All persons, 16 and over in poverty areas	8.6
Black males, 20 and over	8.7
All persons of Spanish origin, 16 and over	8.9
Spanish origin females, 20 and over	10.0
Black females, 20 and over	11.1
All blacks, 16 and over	12.7
All persons of Puerto Rican origin, 16 and over	13.1
White teenagers, 16-19	13.5
All teenagers, 16-19	16.3
Spanish origin teenagers, 16-19	21.0
Black teenagers, 16-19	41.9
Black teenagers, 16-19 in poverty areas of metropolitan areas	47.4

Note: Data are unadjusted.

Figure 32. Major Unemployment Indicators, 1967-76

[Unemployment rates of persons 16 years and over]

Year and month	All civilian workers	Men, 20 years and over	Women 20 years and over	Both sexes, 16 to 19 years	White	Black and other	House-hold heads	Married men	Full-time workers	Part-time workers	Un-employed 15 weeks and over	Labor force time lost
1967	3.8	2.3	4.2	12.9	3.4	7.4	2.1	1.8	3.4	6.9	0.6	4.2
1968	3.6	2.2	3.8	12.7	3.2	6.7	1.9	1.6	3.1	6.5	.5	4.0
1969	3.5	2.1	3.7	12.2	3.1	6.4	1.8	1.5	3.1	6.2	.5	3.9
1970	4.9	3.5	4.8	15.2	4.5	8.2	2.9	2.6	4.5	7.6	.8	5.3
1971	5.9	4.4	5.7	16.9	5.4	9.9	3.7	3.2	5.5	8.7	1.4	6.4
1972	5.6	4.0	5.4	16.2	5.0	10.0	3.3	2.8	5.1	8.6	1.3	6.0
1973	4.9	3.2	4.8	14.5	4.3	8.9	2.9	2.3	4.3	7.9	.9	5.2
1974	5.6	3.8	5.5	16.0	5.0	9.9	3.3	2.7	5.1	8.6	1.0	6.1
1975	8.5	6.7	8.0	19.9	7.8	13.9	5.8	5.1	8.1	10.3	2.7	9.1
1976	7.7	5.9	7.4	19.0	7.0	13.1	5.1	4.2	7.3	10.1	2.5	8.3

Figure 33. Unemployed Persons and Unemployment Rates, by Reason, Sex, Age, and Race, 1967-76

[Persons 16 years and over]

Item	Number unemployed (thousands)						Unemployment rate					
				Entrants		New workers				Entrants		New workers
	Total	Job losers	Job leavers	Total	Reentrants		Total	Job losers	Job leavers	Total	Reentrants	
TOTAL												
1967	3,008	1,229	438	1,341	945	396	3.9	1.6	0.6	1.7	1.2	0.5
1968	2,817	1,070	431	1,316	909	407	3.6	1.3	.5	1.7	1.2	.5
1969	2,831	1,017	436	1,378	965	413	3.5	1.2	.5	1.7	1.2	.5
1970	4,088	1,809	549	1,730	1,227	503	4.9	2.2	.7	2.1	1.5	.6
1971	4,993	2,313	587	2,093	1,466	627	5.9	2.8	.7	2.5	1.7	.7
1972	4,840	2,089	635	2,116	1,444	672	5.6	2.4	.7	2.4	1.7	.8
1973	4,304	1,666	674	1,965	1,323	642	4.9	1.9	.8	2.2	1.5	.7
1974	5,076	2,205	756	2,113	1,441	672	5.6	2.4	.8	2.3	1.6	.7
1975	7,830	4,341	812	2,677	1,865	812	8.5	4.7	.9	2.9	2.0	.9
1976	7,288	3,625	886	2,777	1,895	882	7.7	3.8	.9	2.9	2.0	.9
WHITE												
1967	2,366	987	347	1,033	740	293	3.4	1.4	.5	1.5	1.1	.4
1968	2,226	849	346	1,031	718	313	3.2	1.2	.5	1.4	1.0	.4
1969	2,261	816	357	1,088	767	321	3.1	1.1	.5	1.5	1.1	.4
1970	3,337	1,502	456	1,378	982	396	4.5	2.1	.6	1.8	1.3	.5
1971	4,074	1,923	484	1,666	1,176	491	5.4	2.5	.6	2.2	1.6	.7
1972	3,884	1,709	527	1,648	1,130	518	5.0	2.3	.7	2.1	1.5	.7
1973	3,410	1,357	552	1,501	1,024	477	4.3	1.7	.7	1.9	1.3	.7
1974	4,057	1,795	634	1,629	1,134	495	5.0	2.2	.8	2.0	1.4	.6
1975	6,371	3,570	697	2,105	1,494	611	7.8	4.3	.8	2.5	1.8	.7
1976	5,855	2,972	756	2,127	1,468	659	7.0	3.6	.9	2.6	1.8	.9
BLACK AND OTHER												
1967	642	243	91	308	205	103	7.4	2.8	1.1	3.6	2.4	1.2
1968	590	221	85	284	190	94	6.7	2.5	1.0	3.3	2.2	1.1
1969	570	200	79	291	198	93	6.4	2.3	.9	3.2	2.2	1.0
1970	752	308	93	351	244	107	8.2	3.3	1.0	3.9	2.7	1.2
1971	919	390	103	427	291	136	9.9	4.2	1.1	4.6	3.1	1.5
1972	956	379	109	468	314	154	10.0	4.0	1.1	4.9	3.3	1.6
1973	894	308	122	463	299	164	8.9	3.1	1.2	4.6	3.0	1.6
1974	1,018	411	122	486	308	178	9.9	3.9	1.2	4.7	3.0	1.7
1975	1,459	771	115	572	371	201	13.9	7.3	1.1	5.4	3.5	1.9
1976	1,433	653	130	647	427	223	13.1	5.9	1.2	5.9	3.9	2.0

168

Figure 33 (Cont.)

[Persons 16 years and over]

| | Number unemployed (thousands) | | | | | | Unemployment rate | | | | | |
| | | | | Entrants | | | | | | Entrants | | |
Item	Total	Job losers	Job leavers	Total	Reentrants	New workers	Total	Job losers	Job leavers	Total	Reentrants	New workers
BOTH SEXES, 16–19 YEARS												
1967	859	151	94	614	297	317	13.1	2.3	1.4	9.3	4.5	4.8
1968	839	130	97	611	281	330	12.7	1.9	1.5	9.0	4.2	4.8
1969	853	126	101	625	294	331	12.2	1.8	1.5	9.0	4.2	4.8
1970	1,105	200	126	780	379	401	15.3	2.8	1.6	10.7	5.2	5.5
1971	1,257	232	116	909	409	500	16.9	3.1	1.6	12.2	5.5	5.7
1972	1,302	247	129	926	393	533	16.2	3.1	1.6	11.5	4.9	6.6
1973	1,225	210	145	871	362	509	14.5	2.4	1.7	10.3	4.3	6.0
1974	1,410	278	172	960	432	528	16.0	3.1	1.7	10.9	4.9	6.0
1975	1,752	447	153	1,152	524	628	19.9	5.1	2.0	13.1	6.0	7.1
1976	1,701	384	151	1,166	490	676	19.0	4.3	1.7	13.0	5.5	7.5
MALES, 20 YEARS AND OVER												
1967	1,061	678	165	219	194	25	2.3	1.5	.4	.5	.4	—
1968	993	599	167	227	205	22	2.2	1.3	.4	.4	.4	—
1969	963	556	164	243	216	27	2.1	1.2	.4	.6	.5	.1
1970	1,636	1,065	209	362	318	44	3.5	2.2	.4	.8	.7	.1
1971	2,086	1,384	237	465	409	56	4.4	2.9	.5	1.0	.9	.1
1972	1,928	1,207	245	475	416	59	4.0	2.5	.5	.8	.9	.1
1973	1,594	941	254	399	344	54	3.2	1.9	.5	.8	.7	.1
1974	1,918	1,253	270	394	348	46	3.8	2.5	.5	.8	.7	.1
1975	3,428	2,569	291	569	496	73	6.7	5.0	.6	1.1	1.0	.1
1976	3,041	2,133	315	593	510	83	5.9	4.1	.6	1.2	1.0	.2
FEMALES, 20 YEARS AND OVER												
1967	1,088	401	179	508	454	54	4.3	1.6	.7	2.0	1.8	.2
1968	985	341	167	477	422	55	3.8	1.3	.6	1.9	1.6	.2
1969	1,015	335	171	510	455	55	3.7	1.2	.6	1.9	1.7	.2
1970	1,347	545	214	588	530	58	4.8	1.9	.8	2.1	1.9	.2
1971	1,650	697	234	720	648	71	5.7	2.5	.8	2.5	2.3	.2
1972	1,610	635	262	714	635	79	5.4	2.2	.9	2.4	2.1	.3
1973	1,485	514	276	695	617	78	4.8	1.6	.9	2.3	2.1	.3
1974	1,748	674	314	760	662	98	5.5	2.1	1.0	2.4	2.1	.3
1975	2,649	1,325	369	956	845	111	8.0	4.0	1.1	2.9	2.6	.3
1976	2,546	1,108	420	1,019	896	123	7.4	3.2	1.2	3.0	2.6	.4

Figure 34. Unemployment Rates and Percent Distribution of the Unemployed, by Major Industry Group, 1967-76

Year	Total unemployed	Experienced wage and salary workers		Wage and salary workers in private nonagricultural industries										
		Total	Agriculture	Total	Mining	Construction	Manufacturing			Transportation and public utilities	Wholesale and retail trade	Finance, insurance, real estate	Service industries	Government
							Total	Durables	Non durables					
Unemployment rate														
1967	3.8	3.6	6.9	3.9	3.4	7.4	3.6	3.4	4.1	2.3	4.2	2.5	3.9	1.8
1968	3.6	3.4	6.3	3.6	3.1	6.9	3.3	3.0	3.7	1.9	4.0	2.2	3.6	1.8
1969	3.5	3.3	6.0	3.5	2.8	6.0	3.3	3.0	3.7	2.1	4.1	2.1	3.5	1.9
1970	4.9	4.8	7.5	5.2	3.1	9.7	5.6	5.7	5.4	3.2	5.3	2.8	4.7	2.2
1971	5.9	5.7	7.9	6.2	4.0	10.4	6.8	7.0	6.5	3.8	6.4	3.3	5.6	2.9
1972	5.6	5.2	7.6	5.7	3.2	10.3	5.6	5.4	5.7	3.5	6.4	3.4	5.3	2.9
1973	4.9	4.5	6.9	4.8	2.9	8.8	4.3	3.9	4.9	3.0	5.6	2.7	4.8	2.7
1974	5.6	5.3	7.3	5.7	2.9	10.6	5.7	5.4	6.2	3.2	6.4	3.1	5.1	3.0
1975	8.5	8.2	10.3	9.2	4.0	18.1	10.9	11.3	10.4	5.6	8.7	4.9	7.1	4.0
1976	7.7	7.3	11.7	7.9	4.7	14.4	7.9	7.7	8.1	4.7	8.6	4.4	6.1	4.4
Percent distribution														
1967	100.0	83.6	3.2	73.5	0.6	9.1	26.2	14.2	12.0	3.6	17.6	2.8	14.5	7.1
1968	100.0	83.7	3.1	72.8	.6	9.2	24.7	13.2	11.5	3.4	18.3	2.7	15.1	7.7
1969	100.0	83.8	2.7	73.0	.5	8.3	25.0	13.6	11.5	3.8	18.9	2.6	14.8	8.1
1970	100.0	86.2	2.3	77.0	.4	9.3	29.2	17.6	11.6	3.7	17.9	2.5	14.0	9.6
1971	100.0	85.7	2.0	76.0	.5	8.5	28.0	16.8	11.2	3.5	18.9	2.6	14.1	7.7
1972	100.0	84.4	2.1	74.0	.4	9.2	23.7	13.4	10.3	3.5	20.4	2.8	14.1	8.3
1973	100.0	83.5	2.2	72.5	.4	9.3	21.5	11.5	10.1	3.3	20.5	2.7	14.7	8.8
1974	100.0	85.1	2.1	74.5	.4	9.4	24.4	13.7	10.8	3.1	20.5	2.7	13.9	8.6
1975	100.0	87.9	1.9	78.3	.4	10.2	29.5	18.1	11.4	3.5	18.8	2.7	13.1	7.8
1976	100.0	86.3	2.4	74.4	.5	9.4	23.0	13.4	9.7	3.3	20.6	2.7	14.9	9.4

Figure 35. Work Stoppages in the United States, 1967-76

Year	Stoppages beginning in year		Workers involved		Days idle during year		Percent of estimated total working time		Per worker involved
	Number	Average duration (calendar days)	Number (thousands)	Percent	Number (thousands)		Total economy	Private nonagricultural	
1967	4,595	22.8	2,870	4.3	42,100		0.25	0.30	14.7
1968	5,045	24.5	2,649	3.8	49,018		.28	.32	18.5
1969	5,700	22.5	2,481	3.5	42,869		.24	.28	17.3
1970	5,716	25.0	3,305	4.7	66,414		.37	.44	20.1
1971	5,138	27.0	3,280	4.6	47,589		.26	.32	14.5
1972	5,010	24.0	1,714	2.3	27,066		.15	.17	15.8
1973	5,353	24.0	2,251	2.9	27,948		.14	.16	12.4
1974	6,074	27.1	2,778	3.5	47,991		.24	.24	17.3
1975	5,031	26.8	1,746	2.2	31,237		.16	.16	17.9

Figure 36. Labor Turnover Rates of Employees on Manufacturing Payrolls, 1967-76

[Per 100 employees]

Year and month	Accession rates		Separation rates		
	Total	New hires	Total	Quits	Layoffs
1967	4.4	3.3	4.6	2.3	1.4
1968	4.6	3.5	4.6	2.5	1.2
1969	4.7	3.7	4.9	2.7	1.2
1970	4.0	2.8	4.8	2.1	1.8
1971	3.9	2.6	4.2	1.8	1.6
1972	4.4	3.3	4.2	2.2	1.1
1973	4.8	3.9	4.6	2.7	.9
1974	4.2	3.2	4.8	2.3	1.5
1975	3.7	2.0	4.2	1.4	2.1
1976	3.9	2.6	3.8	1.7	1.3

Figure 37. Reasons for Nonparticipation in the Labor Force, by Age and Sex, 1968-76

Nonparticipants by reason for status	Total								
	1968	1969	1970	1971	1972	1973	1974	1975	1976
THOUSANDS OF PERSONS									
Total	53 289	53 596	54 275	55 662	56 784	57 220	57 586	58 648	59 125
In school	7 007	7 084	7 126	7 615	7 501	7 344	7 187	7 730	7 827
Ill health, disability	4 310	4 453	4 358	4 632	4 945	5 191	5 444	5 461	5 361
Home responsibilities	32 930	32 641	33 088	33 223	33 482	33 188	32 988	32 443	31 957
Retirement, old age	5 510	5 795	5 918	6 160	6 691	7 165	7 379	7 851	8 596
Think cannot get job	667	574	638	774	676	679	686	1 082	910
All other reasons	2 804	3 049	3 145	3 260	3 398	3 652	3 902	4 081	4 474
Males	12 314	12 672	13 065	13 711	14 192	14 539	14 903	15 787	16 341
In school	3 503	3 586	3 618	3 880	3 827	3 762	3 601	3 927	3 929
Ill health, disability	2 119	2 192	2 253	2 390	2 522	2 675	2 828	2 853	2 868
Home responsibilities	176	181	221	241	214	226	237	219	244
Retirement, old age	4 968	5 109	5 216	5 405	5 703	5 927	6 127	6 428	6 816
Think cannot get job	213	183	221	238	240	225	227	359	321
All other reasons	1 335	1 420	1 534	1 557	1 688	1 725	1 882	2 001	2 163
Females	40 975	40 924	41 210	41 951	42 591	42 681	42 683	42 861	42 784
In school	3 504	3 498	3 508	3 735	3 674	3 582	3 586	3 803	3 897
Ill health, disability	2 221	2 261	2 105	2 242	2 424	2 516	2 616	2 608	2 494
Home responsibilities	32 754	32 461	32 867	32 982	33 269	32 962	32 751	32 224	31 713
Retirement, old age	572	686	703	755	989	1 238	1 251	1 423	1 780
Think cannot get job	454	391	417	536	526	454	459	722	590
All other reasons	1 468	1 628	1 610	1 702	1 710	1 928	2 019	2 080	2 311

Nonparticipants by reason for status	Total								
	1968	1969	1970	1971	1972	1973	1974	1975	1976
THOUSANDS OF PERSONS									
Total	53 289	53 596	54 275	55 662	56 784	57 220	57 586	58 648	59 125
PERCENT DISTRIBUTION									
Total	100 0	100 0	100 0	100 0	100 0	100 0	100 0	100 0	100 0
In school	13 1	13 2	13 1	13 7	13 7	12 8	12 5	13 2	13 2
Ill health, disability	8 1	8 3	8 0	8 3	8 7	9 1	9 5	9 3	9 1
Home responsibilities	61 8	60 9	61 0	59 7	59 0	58 0	57 3	55 3	54 0
Retirement, old age	10 4	10 8	10 9	11 1	11 8	12 5	12 8	13 4	14 5
Think cannot get job	1 3	1 1	1 2	1 4	1 3	1 2	1 2	1 8	1 5
All other reason	5 3	5 7	5 8	5 9	6 0	6 4	6 8	7 0	7 6
Males	100 0	100 0	100 0	100 0	100 0	100 0	100 0	100 0	100 0
In school	28 4	28 3	27 7	28 3	27 0	25 9	24 2	24 9	24 0
Ill health, disability	17 2	17 3	17 2	17 4	17 8	18 4	19 0	18 1	17 6
Home responsibilities	1 4	1 4	1 7	1 8	1 5	1 6	1 6	1 4	1 5
Retirement, old age	40 3	40 3	39 9	39 4	40 2	40 8	41 1	40 7	41 7
Think cannot get job	1 7	1 7	1 7	1 7	1 9	1 5	1 5	2 3	2 0
All other reasons	10 8	11 2	11 7	11 4	12 0	11 9	12 6	12 7	13 2
Females	100 0	100 0	100 0	100 0	100 0	100 0	100 0	100 0	100 0
In school	8 6	8 5	8 5	8 9	8 6	8 4	8 4	8 9	9 1
Ill health, disability	5 4	5 5	5 1	5 3	5 7	5 9	6 1	6 1	5 8
Home responsibilities	79 9	79 3	79 8	78 6	78 1	77 2	76 7	75 2	74 1
Retirement, old age	1 4	1 7	1 7	1 8	2 3	2 9	2 9	3 3	4 2
Think cannot get job	1 1	1 0	1 0	1 3	1 2	1 1	1 1	1 7	1 4
All other reasons	3 6	4 0	3 9	4 1	4 0	4 5	4 7	4 9	5 4

Figure 38. Median Years of School Completed by the Civilian Labor Force, by Sex and Age, 1967-76

Sex and date	16 and 17 years	18 to 24 years	25 to 34 years	35 to 44 years	45 to 54 years	55 to 64 years	65 years and over
BOTH SEXES							
March 1967	....	12.5	12.5	12.3	12.1	10.8	9.0
March 1968	....	12.5	12.5	12.4	12.2	11.1	9.3
March 1969	....	12.5	12.6	12.4	12.3	11.4	9.3
March 1970	....	12.6	12.6	12.4	12.3	11.8	9.6
March 1971	10.4	12.6	12.7	12.4	12.3	12.0	9.9
March 1972	10.4	12.5	12.7	12.4	12.3	12.1	10.2
March 1973	10.4	12.6	12.7	12.5	12.4	12.1	10.5
March 1974	10.4	12.6	12.8	12.5	12.4	12.1	10.9
March 1975	10.5	12.7	12.8	12.6	12.4	12.2	11.7
March 1976	10.5	12.6	12.9	12.6	12.4	12.3	12.0
MALES							
March 1967	....	12.4	12.5	12.3	12.1	10.4	8.9
March 1968	....	12.4	12.5	12.4	12.2	10.6	9.0
March 1969	....	12.5	12.6	12.4	12.2	10.9	9.0
March 1970	....	12.5	12.6	12.4	12.3	11.2	9.1
March 1971	10.4	12.6	12.6	12.5	12.3	11.5	9.6
March 1972	10.4	12.6	12.7	12.5	12.3	11.9	10.1
March 1973	10.4	12.6	12.7	12.0	12.4	12.1	10.7
March 1974	10.4	12.6	12.8	12.6	12.4	12.1	11.8
March 1975	10.5	12.6	12.9	12.6	12.4	12.1	12.0
March 1976		12.6		12.6	12.4	12.2	
FEMALES							
March 1967	....	12.6	12.5	12.3	12.2	11.6	10.1
March 1968	....	12.6	12.5	12.3	12.3	12.0	10.3
March 1969	....	12.6	12.5	12.4	12.3	12.1	10.2
March 1970	....	12.6	12.6	12.4	12.3	12.1	10.9
March 1971	10.5	12.7	12.6	12.4	12.4	12.1	11.0
March 1972	10.5	12.7	12.7	12.4	12.4	12.2	11.2
March 1973	10.5	12.7	12.7	12.5	12.4	12.2	11.3
March 1974	10.5	12.7	12.7	12.5	12.4	12.3	11.1
March 1975	10.5	12.7	12.8	12.5	12.4	12.2	11.6
March 1976		12.7		12.6	12.4	12.3	12.1

Figure 39. Labor Force Status and Labor Force Participation Rates of Married Women, Husband Present, by Presence and Age of Children, 1967-76

Date	Total	No children under 18 years	Children 6 to 17 years only	Children under 6 years		
				Total	No children 6 to 17 years	Children 6 to 17 years
	Number in labor force (thousands)					
March 1967	15 908	7 158	5 269	3 480	1 629	1 851
March 1968	16 821	7 564	5 693	3 564	1 641	1 923
March 1969	17 595	7 853	6 146	3 596	1 756	1 840
March 1970	18 377	8 174	6 289	3 914	1 874	2 040
March 1971	18 530	8 432	6 424	3 674	1 862	1 812
March 1972	19 249	8 797	6 706	3 746	2 014	1 732
March 1973	19 821	9 107	6 658	4 056	2 268	1 788
March 1974	20 367	9 365	6 792	4 210	2 343	1 867
March 1975	21 111	9 702	6 972	4 437	2 503	1 934
March 1975	21 143	9 718	6 988	4 438	....	....
March 1976	21 554	9 860	7 270	4 424	2 421	2 003
	Labor force participation rate[2]					
March 1967	36 8	38 9	45 0	26 5	26 9	26 2
March 1968	38 3	40 1	46 9	27 6	27 8	27 4
March 1969	39 6	41 0	48 6	28 5	29 3	27 8
March 1970	40 8	42 2	49 2	30 3	30 2	30 5
March 1971	40 8	42 1	49 4	29 6	30 0	29 3
March 1972	41 5	42 7	50 2	30 1	31 1	29 1
March 1973	42 2	42 8	50 1	32 7	34 3	30 9
March 1974	43 0	43 0	51 2	34 4	35 7	32 9
March 1975	44 4	43 9	52 4	36 6	38 7	34 3
March 1975	44 4	43 9	52 3	36 6	....	....
March 1976	45 0	43 8	53 7	37 4	38 5	36 2

[1] Data revised due to computer editing, weighting, and allocation procedures
[2] Percent of noninstitutional population in the labor force

Figure 40. Full and Part-Time Status of the Civilian Labor Force, by Age and Sex, 1967-76

[Numbers in thousands]

Year and item	Full time				Part time			
	Civilian labor force	Employed	Unemployed looking for full time work	Unemployment rate	Civilian labor force	Employed (voluntary part time)	Unemployed looking for part time work	Unemployment rate
TOTAL								
1967	67.465	65.173	2.293	3.4	9.882	9.199	683	6.9
1968	68.332	66.195	2.138	3.1	10.405	9.726	679	6.5
1969	69.700	67.558	2.142	3.1	11.032	10.343	689	6.2
1970	71.019	67.819	3.201	4.5	11.696	10.808	887	7.6
1971	72.078	68.130	3.949	5.5	12.034	10.990	1.044	8.7
1972	74.028	70.259	3.769	5.1	12.513	11.443	1.071	8.6
1973	75.862	72.571	3.291	4.3	12.852	11.839	1.013	7.9
1974	77.807	73.866	3.941	5.1	13.204	12.070	1.134	8.6
1975	79.096	72.659	6.437	8.1	13.517	12.124	1.393	10.3
1976	80.831	74,957	5.874	7.3	13.942	12.528	1.414	10.1

Index